CREDITS

In writing this book it has not always been easy to gather information. The book itself, is intended not so much as a manual, as an invitation to compile a manual. It is hoped that it will be seen as a foundation for a building of information into which the words have been poured, but are still not set.

Our indebtedness to CLIC, (Community Links in Cameras), which has been a pioneer in this field, as an inspiration, cannot be expressed enough.

The co-operation of REMAP, (Rehabilitation Engineering Movement Advisory Panels), and its clients has been invaluable.

It is behoven to thank:

Margaret Langridge, an occupational therapist, who sat the hooded wake of research, and the invisible benefits of whose work we inherited.

Barbara Buchler, who painstakingly worked on the layout of the book, and whose eye, like the archer who is certain of the arrow, shot true at the shuffling spectre of bad prose.

John Phillips, whose idea it was.

We would like to express our gratitude to:

Greater London Arts and Westminster City Council for revenue support.

The Arts Council and the Chase Charity for providing funds for the production of the manual.

The Harvist Trust and the Lord Ashdown Charitable Settlement for grants for the D.T.P. equipment which enabled us to undertake the design and typesetting in house.

And to everyone who has contributed, who have names, but are not named here, and are yet not forgotten.

CONTENTS

LIST OF ILLUSTRATIONS

Anyone can learn skills, what you can't learn is how to be disabled, your disability informs your perspective.

NATALIE MARKHAM

CHAPTER ONE : PHOTOGRAPHY

This book tries to understand photography in terms of positive images of disabled people and their needs. Its purpose is to attempt to move towards an independent practice of photography, both as an occupation and as a means of self-expression.

It is intended as a guide to the selection and adaption of photographic equipment and photographic accessories in black and white still photography for disabled people.

The book looks at particular types of camera and photographic equipment from the point of view of operation and control. It does not look at particular makes, or where it does, it does not look at them in order to recommend them. A camera suitable for one person's needs may not be suitable for another, (this applies equally to other equipment and adapted equipment). Indeed, an exhaustive list of, say, cameras, could not be completed, not just because each person's requirements are different, but because manufacturers' models drop from their lists as suddenly as the text from a computer screen suffering from a virus.

The drawings in this book are of two kinds:

(i)   there are (free) interepretations of drawings by REMAP, (Rehabilitation Engineering Movement Advisory Panels), and other engineers commissioned by clients which have been sent on to us. They range from the basic, (eg., grip for left hand operation of a camera, see p. 37), to the more sophisticated, (eg., bell-crank shutter release, see p. 47)

(ii)   our own drawings to illustrate a possible layout or an idea for an adaption.

The object of the drawings is to demonstrate either how to improve access to both equipment and space or the mechanical advantage there is to an adaption; e.g., how the pressure applied to a camera focusing ring can be multiplied by means of a focusing aid.

An A-Z street atlas is a map of a town. It shows you where to go. It does not show you how to go there. In the same way this book does not give detailed engineering drawings; even when an adaption is illustrated that has been designed for a client. The purpose of the drawing is, like the street atlas, to show where to go, not how.

The controller who works at a cab hire firm sends a cab to take you to your destination; it is not their job to know how to drive a cab.

For detailed information you should write to the relevant REMAP. Even then, the panel may have changed its members, and the only record of a design may be old photographs and no negatives, or there may be no records available at all, or the panel itself may have been disbanded.

From the information presented by the panels, the majority of requests to REMAP are for adaption of cameras and camera supports. There are not many requests from clients for adaption of darkroom equipment. This may be because more people are interested in taking photographs than processing them. It is reflected in the fact that the bias of this book is towards adaptions and supports rather than accessible layout design; both movable space and space to move in. The apparent lack of interest may conceal a statement about lack of access. This view is supported by the fact that no requests were sent on by any panel concerning studio work. This is a large field. The book is only a beginning.

To have an adaption made you could apply to your local REMAP who maybe able to help you or advise you, approach a metal workshop in your area, either at your local college of further education, or a local school. These are normally most helpful and teachers will sometimes involve their students or school children in making the adaption as part of a school project. [See Wheelchair Mounted Camera Support and Equipment tray made in association with a local school for a member of CLIC, (Fig.21).]

Cost

For most disabled photographers, an overriding consideration must be one of cost. On invalidity benefit, even a mini tripod is an expensive piece of equipment. Cheaper alternatives may have to be looked for. Something made from basic materials, such as a bean bag, (see Bean Bags, p.58), may serve the same purpose. If the money is available, there will be a more sophisticated solution. The designs in this book try to keep this important consideration of cost in mind. Fully electronic systems are being developed; on and on. With economy in mind, the designs in this book are on a 'do it yourself' basis. Improvisation is always the keynote, using second hand material where available. For example, designing the motorised enlarger, (p.96), could be achieved either by using a costly electronic system, or with the use of fractional horse power motors, or with variable speed motors, as found on domestic sewing machines.

Sometimes items of equipment are referred to, (eg. an automatic enlarger with motorised movement of lens and complete control from baseboard, see p.93), which are clearly beyond people's pockets. Such equipment, however, may have a place in a community scheme.

What Does Photography Have To Offer?

(i)   it is a career

(ii)   it is a hobby for fun/ recreation

(iii)   it is a means other than words with which to communicate

(iv)   it may be used by disabled people as a means to explore their disability, eg., latent vision

(v)   it is an aid to self-image development

(vi)   it may be used as a 'watchdog' to point out society's failure to make allowances eg., the light button that no wheelchair user can reach

(vii)   to remedy discriminating practices; by, eg., taking passport photographs of disabled people who cannot enter photograph kiosks using their wheelchairs

(viii)   to provide a platform from which to campaign against segregation and invisibility

(ix) it brings people together at clubs and venues with a common interest and a mutual concern.

A practising independent photographer, Phil Ridler, has this to say: 'I have heard it said of photographers that we are just frustrated artists. Certainly, in my case, I will readily admit that I can remember from the age of five years old wanting to be an artist when I grew up. This was hardly surprising when you consider from our hospital beds the only stimulating images we had to view were the reproduction masters that "the picture lady" periodically hung on the walls. It therefore seemed quite natural for me to want to do what these people had done.

But as I grew up the combination of lack of opportunity, lack of encouragement - the adults in my life had other ideas for me - made me realise that it took more than wanting to "do" or "be" something, to do or be it. In addition, my ability to capture realism was restricted because of my refusal to draw with self-discipline. Achievement of the desired result always seemed to me to lack spontaneity. Years later I was to discover that photography could produce the results I wanted both in realism and abstract imagery. It was, however, the spontaneity of photography that was to release my creative energy giving me respite from my disability and from my states of anxiety and depressions, allowing me to find myself.

One of the main uses of photography is to document childhood and family life. People today are able, throughout their lives, to collect a source of images which act as references to help them re-assess past events and the other people in their lives.

The quality of our existence has been greatly increased by virtue of the fact that we can refer back to visual statements. For instance, to be able to refer to the photography of our childhood has a therapeutic value which enhances our sense of self.

When we look back at the photographs of ourselves we are re-valuing ourselves and through our identification with those photographs our identity; especially to be able to re-value and compare physical change is, I believe, of utmost importance. To this end photography should be used to help people "come to terms" with disability and disfigurement. Not only is it important for people with disabilities to do photography to help re-value themselves in their environment, but images taken by disabled people can be used to educate other groups about disability. Photography is therefore an instrument both of self-expression and education.'

Language

The language of disability is an emotive subject. There is no one set of words that suits everybody's requirements. A new vocabulary is needed.

By some, the terms 'impaired person' and 'impairment' are used instead of 'disabled person' or 'disability' on the grounds that disability is not inherent in impairment but is imposed from without. Someone who is impaired is not necessarily disabled; that he/she is, is a social construction. It is society's misperception of impairment which defines it in terms of disability as a negative quality.

By others the terms 'disabled person' and 'disability' are used because the terms 'impaired

person' and 'impairment' make those people uncomfortable. Why is this so? Is it because the term 'impaired' is associated in our minds with not being a 'whole' person?

Such an association is made in the definition of 'impairment' in the section on the 'meaning of disabled people' in the Attenborough Report (1985). [1] The Report points out that: 'there are no universally accepted terms in which to discuss the topic of enquiry', the authors are convinced, however, that: 'the humanity all hold in common is of more fundamental importance than differentiation by reference to physical or mental capacity'.

Yet in spite of this 'humanity all hold in common' the authors immediately proceed to segregate by use of their definitions. Impairment is defined: 'Any loss or abnormality of psychological, physiological or anatomical function.'

This recalls the painter who said: 'I had my lower right leg amputated in February and it hasn't affected my creativity.' [2]

The unwitting assumption is that an 'impaired person' is not a whole person.

CHAPTER TWO : ORGANISATIONS

CLIC

(Community Links in Cameras)

CLIC is a photography group of disabled people. It organises and runs informal photography workshops based on the ideas and interest of its members who have ranging degrees of photographic experience.

The idea of the group came from women resident at the Convent of St Mary Edgwood who approached Maria Bartha of CRAB, (Community and Recreational Arts in Barnet, Avenue House, East End Rd, London N3 3QE. Tel: 081 346 9189), to help with the organisation of 'on-location' photography workshops.

As the group grew, it became necessary to search for a space with a wheelchair accessible community darkroom. The search came to an end when Hendon College of Adult Studies, Flower Lane offered CRAB a disused, dilapidated shower block. The designing and building of the darkroom took over a year with the help of disabled and able-bodied people. As Maria Bartha of CLIC observes: 'What is important in such a project is for disabled people to be involved at every stage of production, whatever it is.'

The darkroom, however, had many drawbacks to its use. It was too small. It could accommodate only two wheelchair users at a time. It was closed for twenty-two weeks of the year.

At the end of 1988, CLIC and CRAB launched as a joint venture, Community Focus, which is London's first fully accessible darkroom/studio at Tedder Lounge, Grahame Park Way, London, NW9 5UD. Tel: 081 200 8353.

Community Focus is a workspace designed and adapted to meet the requirements of disabled people. It has professional equipment which has been purchased from self-raised funds. It is intended that the darkroom and studio should be available to the residents of Grahame Park and to local schools. CRAB's three photography workers offer assistance and advice to help develop the use of the resource. Photography workshops are not exclusively camera based, but also give practical guidance in picture-making without a camera such as how to produce sun pictures and photograms.

CLIC also organises touring exhibitions. A recurrent theme in the group's photography is the transmission of active, positive images of disabled people. Its members visit exhibitions, attend lectures and workshops and give talks about their own work. 'Through active participation in photography CLIC members educate and inform the public which will eventually change their attitude towards disabled people,' (Maria Bartha).

The Disabled Photographers' Society
P.O. Box 41
Wallington
Surrey SM 9SG
In its information sheet the Society states that it provides advice, instruction, cameras and darkroom equipment to disabled people, enabling and encouraging them to enjoy photography as a leisure and therapeutic activity.

The Society no longer offers to supply adaptions for its members because there are, in its view, others who are better equipped to undertake such manufacturing processes. The society is however happy to consult members on such matters.

The Disabled Photographers' Society has members all over the UK who keep in touch with each other via a regular newsletter. There is an annual exhibition. Membership is open to registered disabled people only. The subscription is, at time of writing, £4.00 per annum for individual members and £10.00 per annum for groups.

The Society solicits donated cameras and equipment which are then checked over before being given to hospitals, day centres, colleges, schools for disabled people and individual disabled people. Indeed, one benefit of becoming a member of the Society is that, as a result of a recent successful Radio Four Appeal, the Society has a stock of donated cameras, enlargers and darkroom equipment.

The Society has a resident camera 'wizard' who will rectify, where they are rectifiable, faults found in these cameras. Another member of the Society, due to his long association with the Royal Hospital and Home in Putney, is responsible for working with skilled technicians there to see what adaptions can be devised when need arises. Another benefit of becoming a member of the Society is film at special prices. The prices of this film, due to the sponsorship of the Society by Konica, are well below those to be found in the shops.

REMAP

(Rehabilitation Engineering Movement Advisory Panels)
REMAP is part of RADAR (The Royal Association For Disability and Rehabilitation),
25 Mortimer St.,
London. W1N 8AB.
Tel: 071 637 5400

Twenty years ago, Pat Johnson, an engineer, formed a panel of engineers, handypeople and others who set about designing and supplying specialised aids for disabled people.

REMAP is a national network of some 2000 volunteers making up panels of engineers, handypeople, occupational therapists. Half the national membership is engineers supported by carpenters, machinists, etc. The other half is composed of occupational therapists, physiotherapists, social workers, doctors. A panel usually has some fifteen members, half engineers of various backgrounds, some four or more occupational therapists. Each panel has one or more handypeople who can make up and modify 'one-off' aids. Panels 'run their own show'. They are independent of one another. They elect their own chairperson and secretary.

Panel meetings are usually monthly to review the progress of existing projects, receive new cash and allocate for design and action. Normally two members undertake responsibility for the problem: an engineer and an occupational therapist. A client is invariably visited to discuss the problem 'on-site'.

Clients are not asked to pay for labour or for materials.

Fig. 1

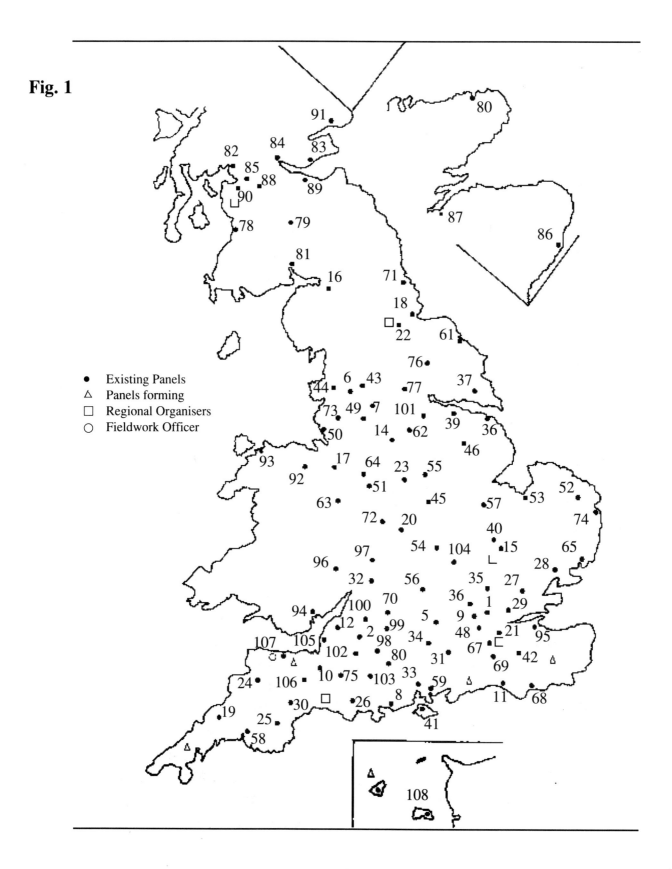

Existing Panels
Panels forming
Regional Organisers
Fieldwork Officer

Members are volunteers. They use unwanted or discarded industrial materials and receive practical help from the government, engineers and apprentice schools and workshops, polytechnics, etc.

There are some 90 REMAP panels throughout England Scotland and Wales. There are a few centres of population not within distance of a panel. Members are not expected to travel outside a radius of 15 miles from base. Consequently until there are more panels REMAP is not able to help every case. [1]

Fig. 1 is a map of the country showing location of REMAP panels and regional organisers.[2] Names and addresses of panel chairpersons and secretaries are obtainable from the National Organiser REMAP.

Location of REMAP Panels and Regional Organisers
England
1. Barnet
2. Bath
5. Berkshire
6. Blackburn, Hyndburn & Ribble Valley District
7. Bolton, Bury & Rochdale
8. Bournemouth
9. Brent & Harrow
10. Bridgewater & District
11. Brighton & District
12. Bristol
14. Buxton & District
15. Cambridgeshire South
16. Carlisle & District
17. Cheshire
100. Chippenham
18. Cleveland
19. Cornwall
20. Coventry & Warwickshire
21. Croydon
22. Darlington & District
23. Derby, Buxton & District
24. Devon North
25. Devon South
101. Doncaster
26. Dorchester (West Dorset)
27. Essex Central
28. Essex North East (Colchester)
29. Essex West (Romford)
30. Exeter & District
102. Frome
32. Gloucestershire
33. Hampshire (Southampton)
34. Hampshire North West (Basingstoke)
96. Hereford
35. Hertfordshire North
36. Herfordshire South
37. Humberside North (Hull)
38. Humberside South East (Grimsby & District)

39. Humberside South West (Scunthorpe & District)
40. Huntingdon
41. Isle of Wight
108. Jersey
42. Kent West
43. Lancashire North East
44. Lancashire North West
45. Leicestershire
46 Lincolnshire North
48. London West (Ealing, Hammersmith & Hounslow)
49. Manchester
99. Marlborough
95. Medway & Swale
50. Merseyside
51. Mid-Staffordshire
104. Milton Keynes
107. Minehead
52. Norfolk Central
53. Norfolk West
54. Northamptonshire
55. Nottinghamshire
56. Oxfordshire & Thames Valley
57. Peterborough & District
58. Plymouth
59. Portsmouth & S. E. Hants
60. Salisbury
61. Scarborough
103. Shaftesbury
62. Sheffield & Rotherham
63. Shropshire (Salopian)
64. Staffordshire North
65. Suffolk East

67. Surrey
68. Sussex East
69. Sussex West (Crawley & District)
70. Swindon & District
106. Taunton
98. Warminster
71. Wearside & District
72. West Midlands (Birmingham)
105. Weston-super-Mare
73. Wigan
97. Worcester
74. Yarmouth & Lowestoft
75. Yeovil & District
76. York
77. Yorkshire West

Scotland

78. Ayrshire
79. Borders Region
80. Caithness & Sutherland
81. Dumfries & Galloway
82. Dumbartonshire
83. Fife
84. Forth Valley
85. Glasgow
86. Grampian Region
87. Inverness
88. Lanarkshire
89. Lothian (Edinburgh)
90. Renfrewshire
91. Tayside

Wales

92. Clwyd
93. Gwynedd
94. Newport, Gwent

The City Of London Polytechnic

11 Houndsditch
London EC3A 7BU
Tel: 071 283 1030

The City Poly has a community liaison programme and offers a Design Surgery for disabled people who need practical help in making or adapting an aid. You can bring an idea for an aid or an aid itself for adaption, or simply go for a chat.

The Design Surgery is 'open-ended'. After the first two diagnostic weeks, participants either enroll on the Basic Programme or are advised regarding enrolment on other HEARU programmes which cover design problems in greater depth.

The course is open to anyone with the interest. No previous practice/skills are necessary. Family and friends are welcome. Check for details.

HEARU

Handicapped Education and Aid Research Unit,
Walburgh House, 56 Bigland St.,
London. E1 2NG.
Tel: 071 283 1030.

HEARU is part of City of London Poly. It is a teaching workshop in individually made aids for disabled people using simple adaptable designs. When an aid develops to a stage where it is potentially marketable, HEARU will advise the designer on his/her interests.

Special rates are available for disabled people. All fees are subject to amendment. Materials are charged at cost price.

Disabled Living Foundation

Living Centre
380 Harrow Rd
London W9 2HU
Tel: 071 289 6111.

The Disabled Living Foundation is a design centre offering adapted equipment for the home. It has a specialist library to which there is chairlift access. The Foundation is a good place for window shopping for ideas and auxiliary aids. Items are often expensive and there is not much on offer for photography.

Other Organisations

In spite of cutbacks, if you need an adaptation for photographic equipment it may well be worth approaching your local engineering workshop, polytechnic, or metal work department of a school.

British Database On Research Into Aid For The Disabled (B.A.R.D)

*Handicapped Persons
Research Unit
Newcastle upon Tyne Poly
No 1 Coach Lane Campus
Newcastle upon Tyne
Tel: 091 235 58211*

B.A.R.D lists details of current or recent UK research on prototypes, design and development of equipment and 'one-off' devices for disabled people. B.A.R.D is regularly updated. Their aim is to collect data on aids for disabled people that are not generally commercially available.

Keith Johnson and Pelling

*93-103 Drummond St
London. NW1 2HJ
Tel: 071 380 11440*

Keith Johnson stocks Bowens/Manfrotto 'Magic Arm' and clamp which can be used in conjunction with a wheelchair.

In Court Sports Ltd

*26 Laurel Park
St Arvans
Chepstow Gwent
NP6 6ED
Tel: 02912 71184*

In Court Sports make an A Frame camera stand with neck harness. (See Mobilia, pp.69-70).

Climpex Ltd

*Hammers Lane
Mill Hill London
NW7 4DY
Tel: 081 959 1060*

Climpex make a system of clamps and rods from which supports can be constructed.

Keith Johnson and Pelling, In Court Sports Ltd, Climpex Ltd, together with a firm called 'Mobilia', (see pp.69-70), all give discounts to members of the Disabled Photographers' Society.

Hugh Steeper (Roehampton) Ltd.

237 Roehampton Lane,
London SW.15.
Tel: 081 788 8165.

Hugh Steeper make orthopaedic aids. They will, however, consider making 'one-off' adaptions on a commercial basis.

SCEPTRE

The Sheffield Centre for Product Development and Technological Resources
Sheffield City Poly, Pond St,
Sheffield S1 1W13
Tel: 0742 20911
Exts 25, 18, 19, 20

Sceptre is concerned with the assessment of socially useful products suitable for production in Sheffield and South Yorkshire. They will make 'one-off' adaptions or will try to solve a problem you have with a piece of equipment, (see solution to recurring cable breakage on pistol-grip, p.37).

Kennett Engineering

The Lodge Works,
Drayton, Parslow,
Nr Milton Keynes,
Bucks. MKT7 0JT
Tel: 029 672 605

Kennett Engineering is a small company based in Milton Keynes. A Clic member has found the staff to be very helpful and they will always try to make a 'one-off' aid.

Photographic Societies

(i)   British Institute of Professional Photography

Fox Talbot House,
Amwell End, Ware,
Herts. S912 9HN
Tel: 0920 464011

(ii)   National Centre of Photography, (see p.28)

Royal Photographic Society
The Octagon,
Milson St,
Bath. BA1 1DN.
Tel: 0225 66841

Disabled Living Centres

Disabled Living Centres have been set up to exhibit aids and provide information. Visitors should always contact a centre before visiting, as an appointment is usually necessary.

A.L.A.C. Disabled Living Centre
Musgrave Park Hospital
Belfast BT9 7JB.
Tel: 0232 669501 Ext. 560

Disabled Living Centre
260 Broad Street
Birmingham B1 2HF
Tel: 021 643 0980

Disabled Living Centre
Caerbragdy Industrial Estate
Bedwas Road
Caerphilly
Mid Glamorgan CF8 3SL
Tel: 0222 887325/6

South Lothian Disabled Living
Centre
Astley Ainslie Hospital
Grange Loan
Edinburgh EH9 2HL
Tel: 031 447 6271 Ext. 241

William Merritt Centre
St Mary's Hospital
Armley Leeds LS12 3QE
Tel: 0532 793140/ 790121

Traids
76 Clarendon Park Road
Leicester LE2 3AD.
Tel: 0533 700747/8

Merseyside Disabled Living
Centre
Youens Way,
off East Prescott Road
West Derby
Liverpool 14 2EP
Tel: 051 228 9221

Disabled Living Foundation Aid
Centre
380 Harrow Road
London W9 2HU
Tel: 071 289 6111

Disabled Living Services
4 St Chad's Street
Cheetham
Manchester M8 8QA
Tel: 061 832 3678/9

The Dene Centre
Castles Farm Road
Gosforth
Newcastle Upon Tyne NE3 1PH
Tel: 091 2840480

Independent Living Centre
108 The Moor
Sheffield SW1 4DF
Tel: 0742 737025

Southampton Disabled Living
Centre
Southampton General Hospital
Southampton SO9 4XY
Tel: 0703 777222 Ext. 3414

Stockport Disabled Living Centre
St Thomas' Hospital
Stockport SK3 8BL
Tel: 061 480 7201 Ext. 15

Swindon Disabled Living Centre
The Hawthorn Centre
Crickdale Road
Swindon, Wilts SN2 1AF
Tel: 0793 643966

Other Centres
Disabled Living Centre
8 Queen Street
Blackpool Lancs.
Tel: 0253 21084 Ext. 1

Bettman Assessment Centre
10 Bettman Close
Cheylesmore
Coventry Warwickshire
Tel: 0203 505066

Aid and Assessment Centre
1 St Giles Street
Netherton
Dudley West Midlands
Tel: 0384 55433

Cleveland A.H.A.
Rehabilitation Information Centre
Middlesborough General Hospital
Ayresome Green Lane
Middlesborough
Cleveland TS5 5A2
Tel: 0642 813133 Ext. 133

Disabled Living Centre
Newcastle Council for Voluntary
Service
The Brampton
Newcastle Under Lyme
Staffs.
Tel: 0782 634949

Disabled Living Centre
Community Service Centre
Queen Street
Paisley Strathclyde
Tel: 041 887 0597

Community Organisations and Projects

The following is a short list of organisations which claim to have accessible photography workspaces and/or adapted darkrooms. It is not comprehensive and includes only those organisations that have responded to our enquiries. The word 'adapted' is often used, unthinkingly, as a euphemism. What does it mean, for example, when somebody says that a bench and sink are at a 'reasonable' level? We understand accessible 'with assistance' to mean not accessible, as when it is stated that: 'the needs of individuals will be considered carefully.' It has not been possible to check details for accuracy and, since there is no hard and fast definition of what 'adapted' means, there will be considerable variation in standards.

We would recommend that you contact your local Arts Centre, Adult Education Institute etc., to see what facilities they have.

The Arts Council publish two Directories which may be useful:

(i)   Arts and Disability Organisations and Projects (1989)

(ii)   Independent Photography (1986)

These may be obtained through the Arts Access Unit and the Photography Unit of:

*The Arts Council
14 Great Peter Street,
London. SW1 3NQ
Tel: 071 333 0100.*

The Arts Council has also published a report: 'Photography and Disability in England', (1990), which investigates the practice and potential of photography and disability in England.

The Arts Council will also be able to put you in contact with your regional arts association.

(1)   Arts Integration Merseyside, (AIM), Mount Vernon Green, Liverpool 17. Tel: 051 709 9988.

Arts Integration Merseyside is an arts organisation of disabled people which exists to encourage the active involvement of disabled people in the Arts. The resource has an accessible darkroom with two Durst enlargers. There is also a mobile photography unit.

The continued existence of AIM 'has been jeopardised by the withdrawal of its major funder.' [3]

(2) Oldham Art Gallery, 70 Union Street, Oldham. OL1 1DN.
Tel: 061 678 4651.

Oldham Art Gallery has a continuous programme of photography exhibitions and workshops. There are workshops for disabled photographers.

(3) Action Factory Community Arts, Simmond Street, Blackburn,Lancs. BB2 1AX
Tel: 0254 679335.

The building is fully accessible and has a lift to the first floor. There are black and white photographic resources: two enlargers, processing equipment, cameras, slide projector and screen. The darkroom can accommodate two wheelchair users.

(4) Untitled Photographic Gallery and Workshops, 1 Brown Street, Sheffield. S1 2B5
Tel: 0742 725947.

There is no access to the darkroom which is on the first floor. Installation of a lift is being considered. There is access to the gallery and restaurant. There is a beginners and an advanced workshop on black and white photography and a workshop on 'issues'.

(5) Kirklees Art Space, Society Eastthorpe Gallery, Huddersfield Road, Mirfield, West Yorkshire WF14 8AT. Tel: 0924 497646.

There is access to the building on both floors. There are workshops for disabled people. The darkroom has three black and white and one colour enlarger.

(6) The Pavillion, 235 Woodhouse Lane, Woodhouse Moor, Leeds 2. Tel: 0532 431749.

The Pavillion is a women's community Arts Centre which specialises in photography. There is a disabled worker. The darkroom is accessible but equipment is not adapted, though adaption of equipment would be considered if the need arises. Any disabled woman in the area is welcome to participate in the workshop's activities.

(7) Bradford Community Arts Centre. The Old Quaker School, 17-21 Chapel Street, Bradford, Yorks.
Tel: 0274 721372.

The building is fully accessible. In the darkroom there is a Leitz Focomat which can be operated by wheelchair users and people with restricted arm movement. The other enlargers have height control on the baseboard. Sinks, bench, switches, etc., are not adapted.

(8) Byker Photographic Workshop, 26 Arrowby Way, Newcastle, NE6 2FB.
Tel: 091 265 1632.

The workshop has two purpose built darkrooms equipped for both black and white and colour work. One is specifically designed and equipped for disabled photographers. A studio has been set up on a separate site.

(9) Projects UK, 1 Blackswan Court, Westgate Road, Newcastle NE1 1SG. Tel: 091 232 2410.

The Project has five individual darkrooms, four black and white and one colour and a teaching darkroom. There is a copy room, store, equipment loan facility, etc. The building is fully accessible. There are also plans to adapt some of the photographic equipment.

(10) Derby Community Arts, Woods Lane Centre, 31 Woods Lane, Derby, DE3 3UA.
Tel: 0332 38560/1.

Derby Community Photography has a policy to provide resources for disabled people. There is an accessible darkroom with an enlarger and adjustable bench.

(11) Community Focus, Tedder Lounge, Wiggins Meade, Grahame Park Way, London, NW9 5UD. Tel: 081 200 8353.

Community Focus has equipment for black and white photography:

Enlargers: 2 x De Vere 302 35mm and medium format. One De Vere 504 35mm - 5 x 4 format with Ilford Multigrade 500 Head. One 35mm Motorised enlarger. Film processing facilities.

Studio: Four Multiblitz Minilights 200. Four tungsten lights. 2.4m and 1.2m backdrop papers. All equipment ceiling mounted/suitable for wheelchair users. Drymounting facilities. Cameras: 35mm SLR's / autofocus/medium format/small flashguns/tripods, lenses and other accessories to assist disabled photographers to practice photography as independently as possible.

(12) Camerawork, 121 Roman Road, Bethnal Green, London, E2 0QN. Tel: 081 980 6256.

There is access to the gallery. One darkroom with two enlargers is accessible, as are the toilets and offices. The other darkrooms are down a flight of stairs.

(13) Independent Photography Projects, The Clockhouse Community Centre, Defiance Walk, Woolwich Dockyard, London SE18.
Tel: 081 316 1909.

The Project runs courses and workshops in photography for disabled people. The building has lifts on all floors. The working surfaces in the darkroom, (wet sink, enlarger etc.,), are accessible. The Project has clamps, adaptors for mounting a camera on a wheelchair, etc.

(14) Battersea Arts Centre, Old Town Hall, Lavender Hill, London, SW1 5TF. Tel: 071 223 6557.

The Centre has three darkrooms, one of which has adapted equipment.

(15) Lenthall Road Workshops, 81 Lenthall Road, Hackney, London E8. Tel:071 254 3082.

There is an accessible darkroom. The workshop can provide 'one-to-one' attention. Book ahead. All the workers are women and priority is given to women who wish to use the facilities.

(16) Newham Arts Council, Shed 22, Comunity Arts Centre, Coolfin Road, Custom House, London E16 3BD. Tel: 071 474 8597.

Both building and darkroom are fully accessible.

(17) Chestnuts Community Arts Centre, Chestnuts Recreation Ground, St Ann's Road, London N15. Tel: 081 800 8095.

The facilities, which include a darkroom, are fully accessible.

(18) Watershed Trust, 1 Canors Road, Bristol, BS1 5TX.
Tel: 0272 276444.

There is general access to facilities. There are two darkrooms.

(19) National Centre of
Photography, The Royal
Photographic Society,
The Octagon, Milsom Street, Bath
BA1 1DN. Tel: 0225 62841.

A lift has been installed which
makes the darkroom accessible,
but sink and enlargers are at
standing height. There is at
present no lift to the restaurant
downstairs.

(20) Wrexham Library Arts Centre,
Rhosddu Road, Wrexham, Clwyd,
LL11 1AU . Tel: 0352 2121.

There is a darkroom at the
Arts Centre. There is an
organisation specifically for
Disability/Arts: Cadwyn Clywd
Link, Daniel Owen Centre, Mold,
Clywd. Tel: 0352 58403.

CHAPTER THREE : CAMERAS

When buying a camera don't necessarily buy the cheapest. Decide whether your interest justfies a greater financial outlay, and whether your capabilities match those of the camera, (system), you choose. If they do, it may well be worth spending the extra money.

There are five types of camera considered:

(i)   110 camera

(ii)   35mm compact camera

(iii) 35 mm single lens reflex, (SLR), camera

(iv) Medium format cameras

(v)   Polaroid

Camera types vary enormously in price. A compact camera in some cases can cost less than a lens for a 35mm SLR camera. Very often, it will be possible to choose well from the existing range of equipment. Most needs may be served with only minimal, or no changes necessary. The best way to select a camera is, where possible, to 'test it for yourself,' to see what actually suits you. Any advice is secondary to this.

Weight & Body Dimensions

When purchasing a camera it will be necessary to take into account not simply its performance but also its weight and body dimensions. They both affect camera management. Types of camera vary in weight, though there may be overlap. Camera weight and body dimension can affect the type of support required: straps, monopod, tripod or a mechanical system of support. Where manual operation is not possible, scope for mechanical adaption of the camera may be an important consideration.

For example, a medium format camera such as the Bronica ETRS weighs: 465 gms main body (without battery); 1280 gms with 75mm lens, filmback and waistlevel finder without battery. Typical 35mm SLR cameras such as the Canon T50-T90, A-1, AE-IP range, weigh from 490-800 gms (body only), and a

50mm lens weighs from 180-380 gms. Contrast this with a 35mm compact camera such as the Pentax 200m-70 which weighs 465 gms, (without batteries), or the Canon Sureshot Tele which weighs 400 gms, (without batteries). For this reason it is always worth checking a technical data sheet for the individual specifications of a camera.

Camera Types

110 Camera
This type of camera uses miniature film, (16mm), contained in a sealed cartridge. The camera is easy to load. The film, however, cannot be processed by the user. The camera normally has a direct vision viewfinder. With many models the exposure is also fixed because there is only one shutter speed and lens aperture. Some 110s will take a tele-lens attachment. Many have built-in flash. The flash may cause 'red eye'.

The camera is easy to operate because it only has a shutter release and a film advance control. It is made in different shapes. It is often a wafer shape which, although it makes the camera easy to carry, has been found to be a cause of camera shake. The use of a cartridge has the advantage that you do not have to attach film to take up spool. It has the disadvantages involved with small negatives, (not so easy to read, hold, etc.)

35mm Compact Camera
Most direct vision cameras are designed as self-contained units so that the photographer has to do little more than to 'point and shoot'. This type of camera almost always has autofocus, autoexposure, autorewind and built-in electronic flash.

The Pentax Zoom-70, for example, integrates a 35-70mm power zoom lens, zoom finder and zoom flash. Advanced technology ensures a low failure rate. Through the viewfinder you look directly at the subject which will appear reduced in size.

Advantages
(i)   The controls are easy to use

(ii)   The viewfinder gives a clear bright image

(iii)   The controls are all in one unit

(iv) Light and easy to carry.

Disadvantages

(i)   Easy to get finger or strap in way of lens. You will not see this through the viewfinder.

(ii)   Compact cameras generally have no threaded bush in the camera base and cannot be used with tripods; (but see the Canon Sureshot Series).

(iii) Since the body moulding of most compact cameras is made of plastic there is no way of connecting an electrically operated shutter release to the camera.

(iv) The flash is not very powerful.

Look for a compact camera which has a shutter release which is prominent.

It may also be helpful to look at non-standard types of compact. For example, Vivitar make an 'all weather camera', the Vivitar 50, (520gms), which is styled in a rubber armour with shockproof exterior and raised shutter release button.

Single Lens Reflex Cameras

The SLR camera enables you to see the image formed by the lens when you look through the eyepiece of the camera. This means more accurate viewfinding and focusing. You can preview the effect of the many interchangeable lenses available.

In order to operate manually a 35mm SLR or 120 roll film camera you must be able to perform the following operations:

(i)   push the shutter release

(ii)   use the film advance lever

(iii) adjust the aperture rings

(iv) place cassette in compartment

(v)   attach film to take up spool

(vi) open and close camera back

(vii) press film advance release button at bottom of camera

(viii) turn film until it leaves take-up spool

(ix) to focus (i.e. sight not mechanics)

(x)   change lens

(xi) adjust shutter speed

(xii) operate depth of field preview button

By far the greatest range of lenses available at reasonable cost is made for the 35mm SLR

camera. It is a versatile system that can be built up as time and money allow.

The best way to choose one of these cameras is, as with other cameras, by the 'test it for yourself' method. Depending on your disability, you can compare features such as weight, balance and ease of working finger-tip controls in order to assess whether the detailed design of the camera suits you, or is capable of adaption to your needs.

Many SLR cameras now have electronic systems which integrate camera and lens computers with fully automatic control of all camera and lens operations : autofocus, autoexposure, built-in autoflash, built-in motor drive, film setting, film loading and power rewind. You push the shutter release button and the system takes over focusing, controlling flash operation, exposure and handling film operation from loading to rewind. The camera will do everything except 'press the button' (and load the film).

Some SLR cameras have a built in thumb grip on the back of the casing and an attachable front grip, (e.g. Pentax Program A35mm SLR automatic: 490gms without batteries.)

It would be impossible to recommend any SLR cameras because so much depends on individual requirements. However, one or two may be mentioned. The point is that autofocus cameras such as the Pentax Program A 35mm SLR have electronic systems which take over many of the manual functions listed above.

Otherwise these functions are operated by a number of complex control buttons: self-timer lever, preview lever, lens release lever, film wind lever, shutter speed select button, exposure compensation dial, ISO film speed dial, rewind crank, back cover release knob, shutter dial, shutter release button, autolock button, aperture autolock button, film rewind button, flash pop-up button etc.

Canon, (Canon 90, 800 gms), has introduced an electronic input dial into their range of 35mm SLR cameras. This disposes of separate controls. As a result the layout is uncluttered. On the Canon EOS 650 (650gms), in fully automatic mode, you simply press the shutter release button. The panel on the top of the camera indicates which autofocus mode you are in. The EOS has a rubber grip which is inter-changeable with two other grips.

Advantages

(i)   The 35mm SLR camera enables you to change the lens of your camera and replace it with another of longer or shorter focal length.   Moreover the use of a zoom lens makes fewer lens changes necessary. As a result you can effectively take photographs from the same place, which would otherwise require a change of position, closer to, or, further from, your subject; hence less mobility is required

(ii)   The metering gives you accurate light reading

(iii)   On some of the more expensive SLR cameras information such as correct exposure, focus, shutter speed and f-stop are signalled on the focusing screen

(iv)   There is a large back up of lenses and accessories

Disadvantages

(i)   The camera is electronically and mechanically more complex than other cameras

(ii)   Use of autofocus detection relies on sufficient ambient light and subject contrast. Under certain conditions the camera will select on an object of focus different from the object the photographer has in mind.

Even if you decide to specialise, the 35mm SLR camera probably offers the largest range of lenses and accessories. These make it suitable for any type of photography: portraiture, photo-journalism, candid photography, still-life, wild-life, sport, fashion, animals, etc.

Medium Format SLR Cameras

Medium format SLR cameras have a system of interchangeable lenses, magazines and viewfinders. The interchangeable viewfinder means that you can look into the viewfinder at either eye or waist level. The screen is bigger than the 35mm viewfinder, which makes the subject image easier to look at, and many have a magnifier attachment. The camera is more awkward to hold than the 35mm SLR camera because of body dimension and magazine back. It is outside the reach of most people's pockets.

The most generally used roll film size, (120/620), gives a picture 60mm wide. Most roll film cameras take square pictures 12 to a film. A 60mm square negative is over four times the area of a 35mm negative. The negative is easier to hold, to look at and needs less enlargement. (See section on Viewers and Screens).

Medium Format
Twin Lens Reflex Cameras
(Fig.2)

Twin lens reflex cameras have two lenses of identical focal length mounted above one another on a common panel. You focus and compose the image on a large top-screen. The top lens has an aperture which produces a bright image on the screen. This image, however, is seen the right way up, reversed from right to left.

Advantages
(i)   Unlike the 35mm SLR camera, it can be used at waist or chest level

(ii)   Film size medium format.

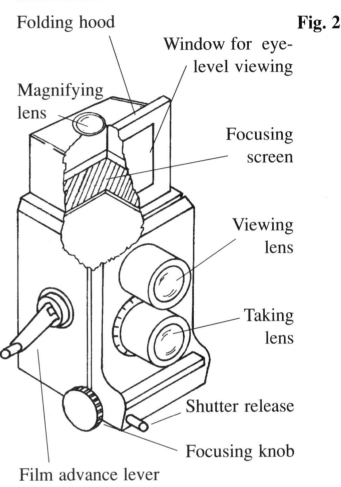

Fig. 2

Folding hood · Window for eye-level viewing · Magnifying lens · Focusing screen · Viewing lens · Taking lens · Shutter release · Focusing knob · Film advance lever

TWIN LENS REFLEX CAMERA

(iii)   It is cheaper than other types of medium format SLR camera

Disadvantages
(i)   Where lenses can be changed, they must be bought in pairs

(ii)   It has no automatic camera movements

Polaroid

Polaroid cameras have a number of advantages, one of which is, that if the instantaneously produced photograph is not satisfactory, another can be taken immediately. There is a black and white film pack available which has a reusable negative. Because of its angular body - it being a camera and a portable darkroom combined - the camera may be awkward to operate. The camera back means that the shutter release control may not always be accessible. However some models have a cable release button and a tripod screw thread. The camera will take flash. It may be worth noting that a Polaroid back can be used with standard medium format cameras. (Types: Impulse: weight 490gms; Polaroid 635: weight 590gms; Image: weight 800gms.)

Non-Standard Cameras

It may be useful to look at specialist non-standard cameras because of the shooting conditions for which they are designed. These conditions will have required alteration to the camera. They may, incidentally, offer an opportunity to serve a need. For example, although there are cameras specially designed for underwater photography with watertight compartments, it is possible to adapt ordinary cameras by fitting them with special underwater housing. (Fig. 3). Because of the conditions, underwater camera controls are simple and enlarged to make them easier to operate. Readouts have to be enlarged because of poor visibility. Film-wind, shutter and aperture release have to connect with large knobs and levers on the outside housing. Such housing could be used under ordinary conditions to

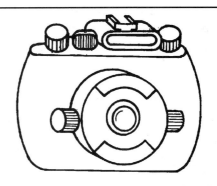

Fig. 3

Most 35mm cameras can be fitted into underwater housings. Camera controls connect to large external knobs and readouts are also enlarged

TYPICAL PROTECTIVE CASING FOR UNDERWATER WORK

Fig. 4

BINOCULAR CAMERA
(Can facilitate sharp focusing)

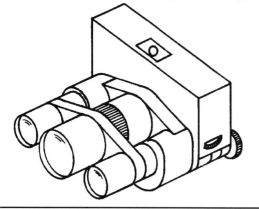

give firm grip, stability and access to controls.

Binocular Camera
(Fig. 4)
The Binocular Camera combines binoculars with a fixed focus 110 camera. It has a limited aperture and shutter speed setting. Some models have interchangeable lenses.

Helmet Camera
(Fig. 5)
Another specialist camera which may be useful, is the helmet camera used by rock climbers. These cameras are mounted on a helmet and often have a separate viewfinder system. They are operated by remote control. However, they are expensive. Adaptions along this idea may prove to be much cheaper.

Fig. 5

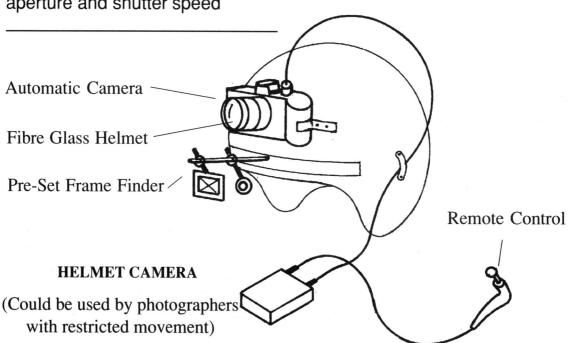

Automatic Camera

Fibre Glass Helmet

Pre-Set Frame Finder

Remote Control

HELMET CAMERA

(Could be used by photographers
with restricted movement)

Cameras That Operate Left Handed

Modern cameras are designed for right hand use of camera. Why does it not enter the heads of camera designers that such discrimination requires a photographer with use of left hand only, to be a contortionist or to operate the camera upside down?

We recently phoned a leading West End camera shop to enquire whether there were any left hand cameras on the market. We were advised that there were not.

We have been informed, however, by Peter Stroud of the Disabled Photographers' Society, that there are cameras on the market which can be operated, (by adaptors), left handed. Peter Stroud comments: 'The shop assistant's response is a characteristic example of the misinformation and lack of motivation on the part of photographic retailers, even specialists.' (For a different view, see Nick Burton, p. 55).

The Konica FT/1 has an electronic terminal at the left side. This can be fitted with a special release button which Konica can supply and the camera will then work left handed. The Konica FS/ 1 and FP/1 work in a similar manner. They are both now discontinued. They can often be found in dealers' second hand stock at a reasonable price. Going up market the Nikon F301, F501 and F 801 all carry an electric terminal to the left. Nikon produce a terminal release adaptor, (the product reference is MR/3), which fits into the terminal and converts the three camera bodies identified above to left hand use. The EXA 500 has a left handed release and the Exacta RTL carries both left and right handed releases. These cameras are also still to be found in second-hand stock. [1]

A pistol-grip trigger (Fig. 19) may be combined with a fully automatic camera to allow use with one hand.

SCEPTRE were requested to solve the problem of recurrent cable breakage due to the fact that the user pressed too hard on the trigger. A heavy duty cable was fitted. (address, p.21).

Left Hand Operation Of Shutter (Fig. 6)

REMAP South Herts [2] was asked to design a grip for left hand operation of a camera. A simple solution, using wood and cord, was reached.

The camera, an Agfa Optima, was secured by a tripod screw to a plain wooden platform which had a central vertical handle underneath.

On this model camera the trigger which operates the shutter is situated at the front of the camera to the right hand side of the lens. It requires a downward pull. A cord, a nylon fishing line, is fixed to the shutter trigger, passed down through an eye screwed into the front of the platform and across the corner, where it is anchored to the central handle.

It will be seen from the drawing that this forms a taut line by means of which the fore-finger of the left hand can operate the shutter trigger.

Second-Hand Cameras

You may find that a camera from second hand stock is more suitable to your needs than a modern camera. Alternatively, you may be able to shop for a new camera or accessory and then by telephoning second-hand shops obtain the same equipment, only much cheaper, and even with a guarantee!

Where the camera thread of a deleted model does not match the tripod screw of a new camera, there are tripod bush adaptors available.

For information on second-hand cameras you could contact, if you are a member, the Disabled Photographers' Society, (address, p.14).

For a list of where to buy camera equipment in London, see *Acknowledgements*, Chapter 3.[3]

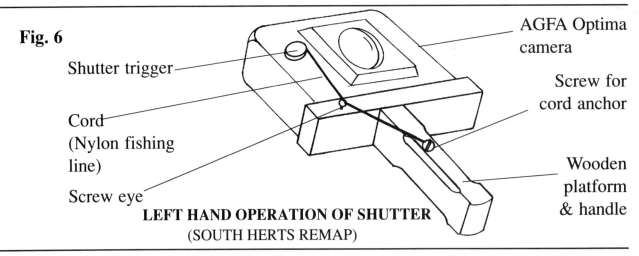

Fig. 6

Shutter trigger

Cord (Nylon fishing line)

Screw eye

AGFA Optima camera

Screw for cord anchor

Wooden platform & handle

LEFT HAND OPERATION OF SHUTTER
(SOUTH HERTS REMAP)

CHAPTER FOUR : ACCESSORIES

Flash

Of accessories, flash is probably the most useful. Many 110 format and 35mm compact cameras have built-in flash.

You can buy automatic computerised flash which you can set to give the correct exposure for most subjects. The unit adjusts the flash to suit the subject distance at the aperture you are using. With a manual flash you have to adjust the lens aperture to control exposure.

You should buy a flash with an adjustable head. Most manual units have fixed heads. If you have a fixed head, there are adaptors for controlling flash angle.

If there is no hot shoe on the camera you will need to hold the flash gun and connect a lead from the flash to a synchronised socket on the camera or to mount the flash on a flash bracket. (See vacuum vari-cushion, p.58).

Cable Release
(Fig.7)

A pneumatic cable release may be used to depress under the chin or under an elbow on a chair arm. For operation by mouth, an ordinary cable release may be used. A soft release is an air-cushioned plunger which when fitted to the shutter release will help control camera shake at slow shutter speeds.

Fig. 7

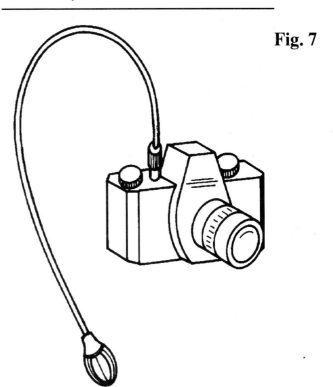

PNEUMATIC SHUTTER RELEASE

Lenses

Telephoto lenses, (85mm to 1200mm), can be long, heavy and difficult to hold steady. Use of a tripod or some other kind of support may be necessary. Catadioptric lenses have focal lengths between 250mm and 2000mm in a short lens barrel. The effect is similar to that of telephotos. However, the catadioptric lens is much lighter and easier to hold steady than many telephoto lenses of equivalent focal lengths. For example, a 500mm telephoto and catadioptric lens have a significant difference in size and weight between them. A telephoto lens can weigh as much as 2500gms, whereas a catadioptric as little as 750gms. A zoom lens, with its variable focal length, allows you to carry fewer lenses. In addition it permits precise framing without changing your viewpoint. A zoom lens is generally lighter than a telephoto.

Macro lenses produce fine quality close-up pictures. You can use them for normal photography but they give their best results close up. Area of sharp focus is shallow. For larger magnifications your lens must be nearer to the subject than the film. For this extension tubes or folding bellows are used. Extension tubes must be used with a tripod.

Viewers And Screens

The pentaprism head, through which the camera image is seen, is a feature of all SLR cameras. Where focusing is critical, photographers may use alternative viewers. The facility for changing these parts is, however, only available on some advanced SLR cameras.

The electronic meter circuitry prevents the removal of the viewing head on autofocus cameras. There are however certain adaptors which can be attached to fixed-head cameras. For wearers of spectacles, prescription lenses can be fitted to the eyepiece. (Fig. 8).

Viewfinder Magnifier
(Fig. 8)

A Viewfinder Magnifier enlarges the image on the screen and is usually used in scientific or close-up work. Enlargement is x6. As with all non-reflex viewers the uncorrected image on the screen is seen reversed, as in a mirror.

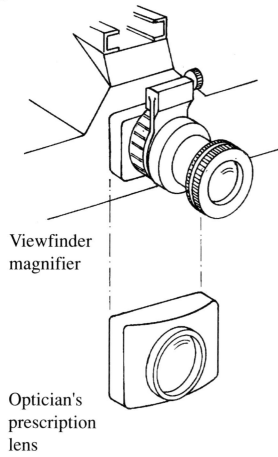

Fig. 8

Viewfinder
magnifier

Optician's
prescription
lens

VIEWFINDER AIDS

Right Angle Finder
A Right Angle Finder is an accessory to the pentaprism not a replacement. By swivelling the eyepiece the camera can be viewed above or from the side.

Waist Level Finder
A Waist Level Finder is useful when the camera cannot be brought to the eye.

Focusing Screens
As with viewing heads, focusing screens can be interchanged only with certain cameras. A comprehensive range is available for advanced SLR manual cameras while screens on certain electronic models can be replaced only by a camera mechanic. A standard screen has split-image centre zone. A screen without split-image is often more suitable for small aperture work as the ring tends to black out under f4.

CHAPTER FIVE : CAMERA ADAPTIONS

Each person's needs are specific. Very often, an adaption suitable for use by one person will be of little use to another because of the shortcomings of the device, (as a result of the particularity of the need for which it was designed).

Where possible, one should look for something currently available on the market which will achieve a specific result without the need for adaption, or which, at least, will go some way to achieving that result. If necessary, it can then be used as a basis for adaption.

For example, REMAP, Salisbury were asked to design a support for a photographer who had use of their right hand. The only solution of the panel was a short monopod suspended from its base by a neck-strap. The crude prototype was made from a short length of broomstick. The monopod had a screw-thread at the top to engage the bush on the camera. This meant that it could only be held in a landscape position.

In fact, there are on the market, several types of monopod with universal joint, (and neck-strap), which makes the portrait position possible.

REMAP Mid Staffs designed a frame to mount an SLR camera on a wheelchair at eye-level without realising at the time that there were commercial equivalents at least as functional.

Because there are commercial equivalents, however, does not mean that it may not be better to have something made up. There is the advantage of individual attention and detailed design; and the support may be much cheaper, or no cost at all.

An idea to be considered would be to compile a database of all photographic accessories currently available which could be used as a basis to specify for individual needs, perhaps along the lines of B.A.R.D. (See p.20). Of course, this would not replace the necessity to indicate specific adaptions.

Camera Adaptions

Brighton REMAP report a chin operated control, (Fig. 9). Tom Yendle, a student without arms, had made himself a camera harness but could not operate the focus and zoom rings while looking through the viewfinder.

The panel devised a system in which soft rubber tyres from a model aircraft were used to turn a toothed belt pulley operating on the lens ring. The camera is operated by a pneumatic cable release. [1]

Fig. 9

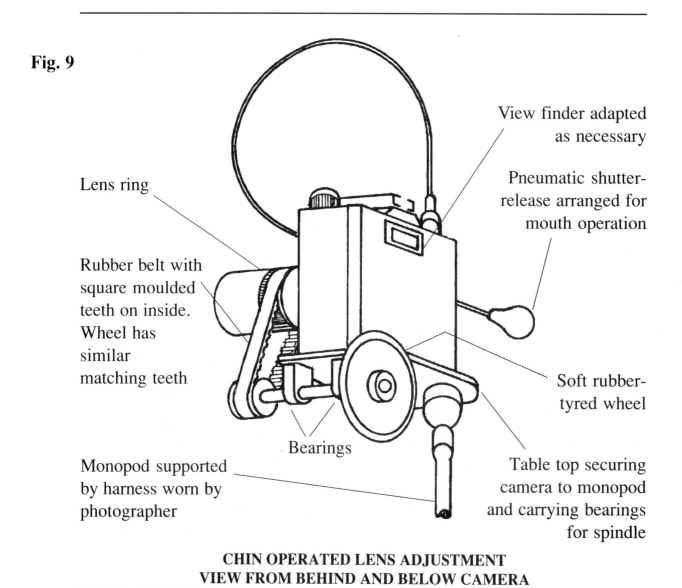

View finder adapted as necessary

Pneumatic shutter-release arranged for mouth operation

Lens ring

Rubber belt with square moulded teeth on inside. Wheel has similar matching teeth

Soft rubber-tyred wheel

Bearings

Monopod supported by harness worn by photographer

Table top securing camera to monopod and carrying bearings for spindle

CHIN OPERATED LENS ADJUSTMENT
VIEW FROM BEHIND AND BELOW CAMERA

Fig. 10

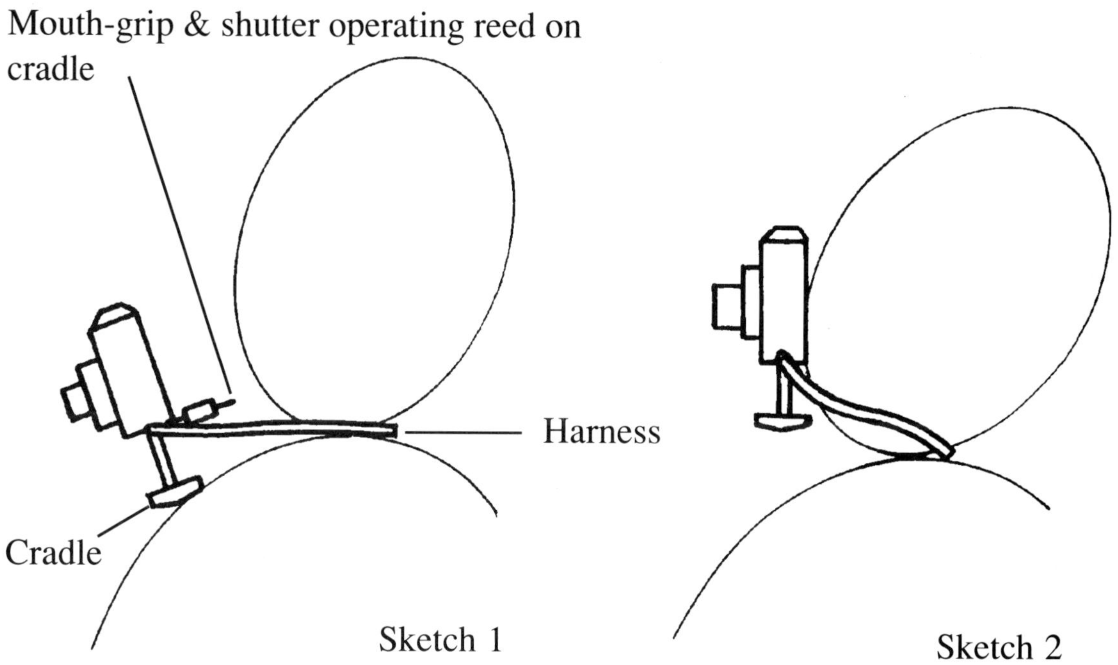

Mouth-grip & shutter operating reed on cradle

Harness

Cradle

Sketch 1

Sketch 2

MOUTH & TONGUE OPERATION OF CAMERA

Knut Aase has designed a kit of parts, (Fig. 10), to enable someone who has no or severe restriction of arm movement to use a camera.

The camera is supported round the neck by a strap after the manner of binoculars.

When the camera is required for use it is raised to face level by means of a moulded mouth grip on the cradle.

The use of a fully automatic camera is assumed needing only the external operation of the shutter release. This is achieved by having a pressure or movement sensitive reed switch built into the mouth grip moulding which can be operated by tongue. [2] (Note: Knut Aase has not provided drawings. Fig. 10, Sketches 1 and 2, is illustrative of his design.)

Focusing Aid
(Fig. 11)

The purpose of this aid is to enable someone who has restricted use of arm/hand movement to turn the focusing ring of a camera.

The aid can be made of alloy strip or plastics. The inner ring is formed as a light fit on the lens focusing ring. To accommodate the pinch-bolt, the ends of the ring are turned up at right angles, with a small gap between them.

The outer ring, larger than the inner ring to give the extra turning

Fig. 12

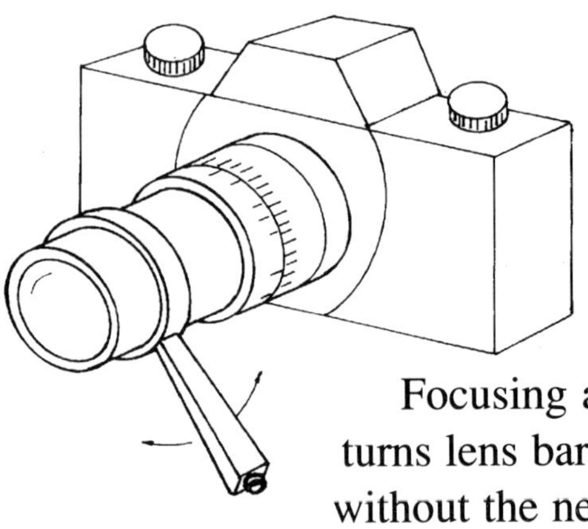

Focusing aid turns lens barrel without the need to grip by hand

**LENS BARREL
FOCUSING AID**
(AICO TYPE)

power, is connected to it by spokes.

An alloy wheel is made from a flat strip rivetted together.

Alternatively, if plastics are used, the plastic sections used for model making are suitable material and are glued together.

Focusing Handle
(Fig. 12)

You can buy a focusing handle. This is a ring with a handle which fits around the lens barrel at an angle of 90 degrees, (Aico Lens Grip). (See Nick Burton, p.53).

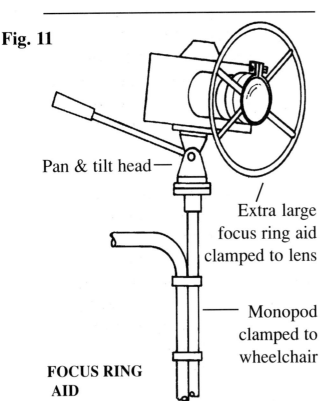

Fig. 11

Pan & tilt head—

Extra large focus ring aid clamped to lens

Monopod clamped to wheelchair

FOCUS RING AID

Fig. 13

LIGHTWEIGHT CONTROLS FOR AUTOMATIC CAMERA

Minolta AF-E11 automatic camera

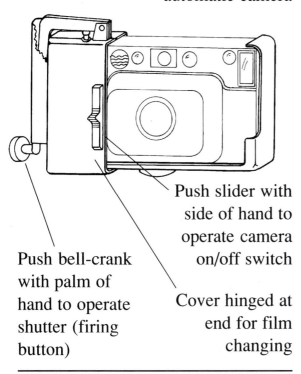

Push bell-crank with palm of hand to operate shutter (firing button)

Push slider with side of hand to operate camera on/off switch

Cover hinged at end for film changing

Lightweight Controls Minolta A.F. E11
(Fig. 13)

REMAP Surrey have designed an adaption for a photographer who could not apply finger-pressure to operate the on-off switch at front of camera or firing button at top.

The object was to provide a means whereby the palm or side of the hand could be used to operate the camera shutter and on/off switch.

The moulded plastic camera body was not strong enough to accept any attachments or modifications.

A half-case or cover for the camera was devised upon which to mount the modifications. This does not interfere with the camera functions and is hinged at one end to open for film changing.

To trip the shutter release, or firing button, a bell-crank is used which both multiplies the hand pressure available and brings the release button to the position where it can be operated with the heel of the hand, while holding the camera in cupped hands.

For working the on/off switch a slider located on the front of the cover engages the switch. It can be operated with the side of the hand.

Fitting a cable release to a compact camera
(Fig. 14)

REMAP North Herts were asked to fit a cable release to a camera to enable a photographer to operate a compact camera , (Canon Sureshot Ace), with teeth and tongue. (See Nick Burton, p. 54).

Fig. 14

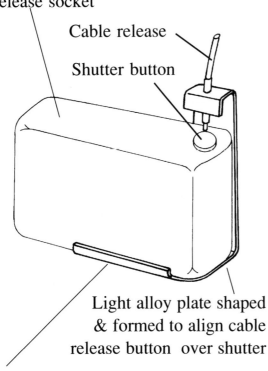

Camera with no cable release socket

Cable release

Shutter button

Light alloy plate shaped & formed to align cable release button over shutter

Secured underneath by tripod screw

CABLE RELEASE MOUNTING

The panel's solution was a sheet alloy plate shaped to fit the sole of the camera and an upright extension which held the cable release in a suitable position to operate the shutter button. This plate was secured to the camera by the tripod screw.

Although this idea was originated for the Canon Sureshot, it could be adapted to any camera which has a tripod bush but no cable release socket.

Solenoid Operated Shutter Release
(Fig. 15)

REMAP Bristol were asked to modify a camera to enable a photographer who was unable to apply finger pressure to the shutter release to take photographs using a wheelchair.

The panel decided upon a solenoid to operate the shutter.

A solenoid is an electrical coil round an iron rod. When the electricity supply is switched on the rod is pulled lengthwise through the coil. If this rod is mounted directly above the shutter button, as in Fig.15, it will fire the shutter.

A control box, the size of a cigar box, contains all the electrical components: battery, on/off switch, capacitor and micro-switch.

The job of the capacitor is to build up the power from the battery so that the solenoid generates a strong pulse when triggered by the micro-switch.

The micro-switch requires only a few grams of pressure to

operate and very little movement. Even so, the operating reed of the switch was made longer for lighter operation. The reed can be seen below the finger hole of the control box.

As with the circuit of a flash gun, an on/off switch has been provided to prevent discharge of the battery when the unit is not in use.

Fig. 15

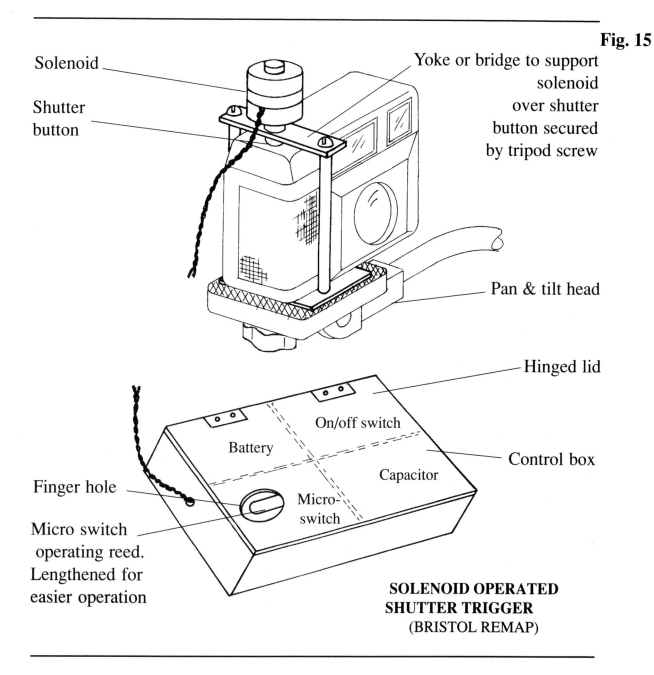

Solenoid

Shutter button

Yoke or bridge to support solenoid over shutter button secured by tripod screw

Pan & tilt head

Hinged lid

On/off switch

Battery

Capacitor

Control box

Finger hole

Micro-switch

Micro switch operating reed. Lengthened for easier operation

SOLENOID OPERATED SHUTTER TRIGGER
(BRISTOL REMAP)

CHAPTER SIX : CAMERA SUPPORTS

Nick Burton, wild-life photographer, relates below how he started photography, and how he has developed his own system of camera supports.

'I have been disabled since September 1974, when, at the age of 16, I sustained a C4/5 dislocation of the cervical spine in a rugby accident. This left me almost completely paralysed from the neck down. However, I have the use of the trapezius, deltoid and biceps muscle groups, which means that I have some restricted movement in my arms, and although I do not actually have any muscular control of my hands, I am able to use them to operate some levers and buttons etc., and to pick up some objects thanks to some 'trick' movements I have learned over the past fifteen years.

I was a patient in The National Spinal Injuries Centre at Stoke Mandeville Hospital for nearly fourteen months, and following my discharge in October 1975, I studied for a degree at home.

Throughout the time I was studying, I tried a number of pastimes including drawing, painting, and jigsaw puzzles. The drawing and painting involved using the pencil or brush held in a leather strap around my hand, which served the dual purpose of supporting my wrist. This is the method I still use for writing. Putting together jigsaw puzzles involved having all of the pieces tipped out on the table in front of me so that I was then able to flip them over at the edge of the table so that they all faced the right way up, (except for the ones I dropped on the floor). I could then sort them into edges and colours, etc. I then assembled the puzzles by sliding the pieces together and connecting them by means of lifting up one side and dropping it into place.

However, none of these my hobbies was able to hold my interest for very long, and in 1984 I began to wonder whether photography would be possible. My first attempts involved using mother's manual SLR camera fitted with a standard 50mm lens which I fired with a standard cable release, held in my mouth.

At this time the camera was supported on the centre column of an old tripod which slotted into a length of copper pipe clamped to the armrest of my wheelchair by two or three jubilee clips. These early attempts were largely unsuccessful, but at least proved that photography should be possible. By this time the photography bug had bitten me hard enough to make me want to keep trying, and a few weeks later, whilst on a visit to Stoke Mandeville, an occupational therapist showed me a brochure for a range of products known as "Orange Aids", (now "Mobilia"), whose agents were Steeper of Roehampton. I went to the Steeper show-room in London where I bought a number of clamps and poles which enabled me to have a further try at photography. The set-up I bought from Steeper consists of the following equipment: a clamp which fits onto the right armrest of my wheelchair, together with a 10mm diameter steel pole which slots into it. This pole rises vertically to a point level with the top of the armrest where it then bends at 90 degrees so as to come across the chair in front of me. There is then another 90 degree bend in the pole so that it then rises vertically in front of me. Onto this fits a flexible metal pole and a ball-and-socket tripod head. These last two items enable the camera to be pointed in different directions.

Using this set-up to support my mother's SLR camera and standard lens worked reasonably well, but the fact that it was a completely manual camera meant that I still needed help to wind on to the next frame and to adjust the shutter speed and aperture settings etc., and so I decided to see what my local camera shop had to offer.

After trying various cameras and equipment in the shop, I bought a Pentax ME Super SLR, together with an electric motor winder and cable release, which I fire by means of holding it in my mouth and pressing the button with my tongue. As my main interest is photographing birds and other wild-life I also bought a Tamron 60-300mm zoom lens which obviously gives a higher degree of magnification when used at the 300mm setting. I am able to focus the lens by means of an Aico Lens Grip, (Fig. 12), which is a kind of lever which fits around the barrel of the lens and protrudes at 90 degrees in such a way that I am able to adjust it with a light touch of the hand. With the ME Super used on its aperture priority setting, the shutter speed is automatically adjusted so as to give an accurate exposure for any given light level. However, there is now a wide range of autofocus cameras on the market which have a variety of exposure programmes and which would obviously make basic adjustments and settings even easier. Due to the very long focal length of the Tamron lens when on its 300mm setting, I generally use it at its maximum aperture which gives as fast a shutter speed as possible, thereby reducing the effects of camera shake to a minimum.

However, this system of camera, motor winder and 60-300mm lens proved to be too heavy for the flexible pole and ball-and-socket tripod head, causing it to tip over very easily. I therefore replaced the flexible pole with another length of 10mm diameter steel pole, on top of which I fitted a fluid-filled

Groschupp tripod head purchased from the camera shop. The weight of the camera, lens and winder is well over a kilogram, however, all of which was in front of the tripod fitting. I asked a friend to make me a bracket made from sheet metal and which holds the camera to the tripod head in such a way that the weight is evenly distributed in front of and behind the camera's point of balance.

This all still proved to be rather too springy, due to the fact that the bent metal pole fitted to the armrest of my chair was only supported from one side, and so I asked my friend to make one final piece of equipment. This consists of an aluminium bar which is long enough to reach right across my chair in such a way that it is firmly supported by both armrests. This bar is connected to the "Mobilia" clamp on the right armrest by means of 10mm diameter steel pole which is screwed permanently to the aluminium bar and is held tight to the clamp when the camera is in use by a separate large-headed screw which is tightened by hand when setting up the equipment. Half way along the aluminium bar, a 10mm diameter hole has been drilled so as to enable the steel pole holding the tripod head and camera to drop into it. This is then held in place by means of a screw which is tightened with an Allen key. This system also allows the height of the camera to be adjusted simply by releasing the Allen key and raising or lowering the pole as required.

In February 1989 I purchased a Canon Sureshot Ace compact camera. At first, I only intended to keep this camera for use by other people so that I could ask them to take a quick photograph of anything I wanted without having to set up all of my SLR equipment. After a while, however, I decided that it was pointless owning a camera and never using it myself. I therefore wrote to the REMAP organisation who put me in contact with Ivor Kemp, one of their engineers, who lives locally. Between us, Mr Kemp and I decided on a design for a device which now enables me to operate the Canon myself, (Fig. 14). The main problem was that like most other modern compact cameras, the Canon Sureshot has no cable release facility. The device Mr. Kemp made consists of a sheet metal bracket which fits over the body of the camera and holds a standard cable release in position over the shutter button in such a way that when the plunger is pressed, the internal 'needle' of the cable release presses the button and fires the camera mechanism. (I hold this cable release in my mouth in the same way as I do for the Pentax). As every other function of the Canon Sureshot is fully automatic, no other modification was needed. The Canon simply fits onto the tripod device described above using the Groschupp tripod's own fittings.

With both cameras, (and incidently, my telescope which I use when bird-watching), I need help to get everything set up, but once this is done, I am free to go and photograph anything I choose, as I almost always use an electric-powered wheelchair which allows me to move around as I please. I also need help to load new films into both cameras. With the Pentax ME Super this involves rewinding the old film manually before opening the back of the camera and removing it. A new film then has to be loaded and threaded through the take-up mechanism. In the case of the Canon Sureshot, (and many other modern cameras), this process is much easier because the old film is automatically rewound, and loading a new one simply involves placing it inside the camera and closing the back. It is then automatically wound to the first frame and the camera is ready for use. Almost anybody who is slightly less disabled than myself and who has some use in their hands would probably be able to operate one of these modern compact cameras with very little difficulty at all.

A wheelchair disabled person who has the use of their hands, but who is unable to support the weight of a camera for very long, or who has difficulty in holding it steady, would perhaps benefit by using a monopod. Most camera shops have a selection of these, many of which are light and very compact and fold away neatly when not in use.

In short, my advice to any disabled person taking up photography as a hobby would be this: decide exactly what you expect from photography, and just what your subject matter is most likely to be, (i.e. children and pets at home, etc., or more distant outdoor subjects such as sports and wildlife). This will have a great influence over the type of equipment you are likely to need. Once you have this clear in your mind, visit your local camera shops. I always prefer specialist shops to the larger chain stores, as they tend to have a greater choice of products, and most importantly, the staff seem to be more knowledgeable.

I have always found the staff in my local camera shops to be very helpful, keen to offer advice and answer any questions, so never be afraid to ask for help. If you need any special modifications to your equipment which cannot be done by your camera shop, and if you do not have a friend or member of the family able to do them, then contact REMAP as I have done. The address of your REMAP co-ordinator can be obtained from RADAR. Alternatively, you could try approaching a local light engineering company to see if they could be of any help.

Above all, enjoy your photography and "If at first you don't succeed, try, try again."

Fig.16

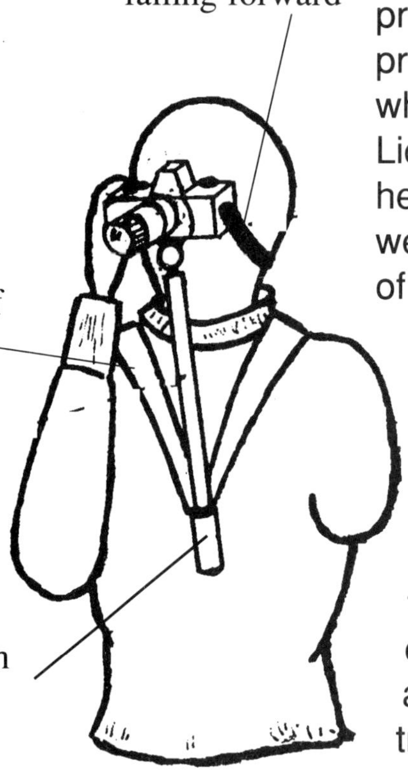

Strap to stop camera falling forward

Strap to take weight of camera

Monopod with ball & socket head

SLING HELD MONOPOD

(CULLMANN MODEL NO. 522
SHOULDER STRAP)

Furthermore, don't expect every frame to be a masterpiece, especially at first; the first 36 exposure roll of film I used only produced six frames which were printable. I once read an article which I think was about Lord Lichfield, in which he stated that he considers himself to be doing well if he gets one frame on a roll of film with which he is happy. If that's good enough for him,

Monopods & Tripods

There are many accessories available to help support a camera or help with the problems associated with camera shake. Among these are monopods and tripods. A tripod is more stable than a monopod, whereas a monopod is lighter to carry and easier to set up; it is not, however, self-supporting. There is no point buying a tripod that is stable only to discover that it is too heavy to transport.

The more adjustable the tripod, the more control you will have. Tripods with braces between the centre column and the legs are generally more stable.

A tripod has a plate with a screw at the top. Heads can be attached by a locking screw. A ball-and-socket or pan-and-tilt head allows you to change camera positions without moving

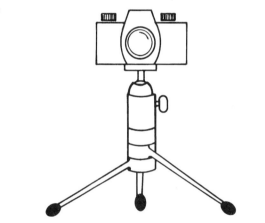

TABLE TRIPOD WITH BALL AND SOCKET HEAD
(LEITZ STYLE)

the tripod.

A mini or table-top tripod is light, and can be used on a wheelchair tray. (Fig. 17).

A suction tripod has a suction pad at base of a column which fixes it securely to any smooth surface. (Fig.18).

When use of a tripod is

Kennett, (address, p.21), make a tripod for 'any photographer working in awkward

situations. The tripod can adjust to any terrain and to any elevation to provide firm support for shots that would normally be considered impossible.' As a result, the tripod can be used by a wheelchair user without the tripod interfering with the wheelchair. 'The swivel head allows independent adjustment of the telescopic legs up to and beyond horizontal whilst also allowing independent adjustment of the centre column elevation.' The head is locked by a lever control. Some people have found this tripod heavy to handle. It is perhaps more suitable for still-life rather than other types of photography, (Kennett Benbo Mkl; Mkll, Baby). [2]

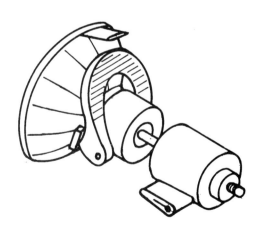

CULLMANN SUCTION TRIPOD
[MODEL NO. 1003]
(attaches to any smooth surface)

Fig. 17

Fig. 18

57

Bean Bags

Bean bags are a cheap and universal tool which you can knock about and massage to your requirements. They consist of a fabric bag filled with dried beans. They are a highly mouldable, accommodating tool, which can take the place of a rigid support. They can, for example, provide a stable base for taking photographs from a car window, or from a tray mounted on a wheelchair, (see Fig. 21), etc.

Vacuum Vari-Cushion

Jessops market a Vacuum Vari-Cushion, as a camera/flash support, for use on rocks, trees, etc. It consists of a synthetic bean bag with an integral vacuum pump. When the air is expelled,

Fig. 19

Fig. 20

Note: both the pistol grip (Fig. 19) and the rifle grip (Fig. 20) can be used right or left handed - or two handed

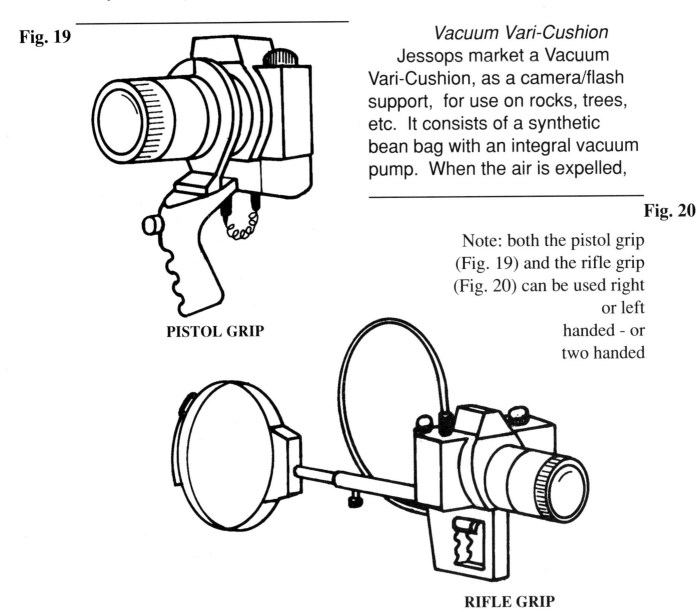

PISTOL GRIP

RIFLE GRIP

it rigidly adopts the shape arranged. Release the vacuum and it becomes pliable.

The cushion is available by mail order, or direct from Jessop Photo/Video Centres.

Jessop of Leicester Ltd.,
Jessop House,
Scudamore Road,
Leicester LE3 1TZ
Tel: 0533 320033.

Straps

Wide straps are useful to spread the weight of the camera, especially if you are using a medium format camera or a camera with a long focus lens.

Dog collar straps with long lugs give more support. Straps should be used that are so made that the buckles cannot run up the strap and pinch the neck.

You can also purchase nylon straps with non-slip padded shoulders which do not have buckles. They are adequate for carrying an SLR camera.

Cullmann make a monopod in conjunction with a shoulder strap, [Model 741(Monopod) in conjunction with Cullmann No. 522 Shoulder Strap,] (Fig. 16).

Jessop make: a heavy duty Braided Camera Strap with nylon

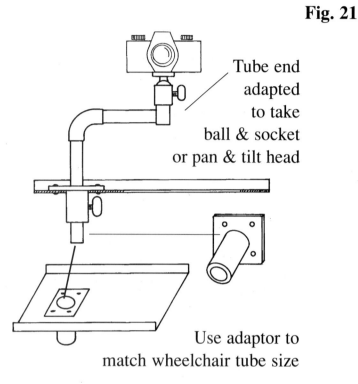

Fig. 21

Tube end adapted to take ball & socket or pan & tilt head

Use adaptor to match wheelchair tube size

TRAY WITH CAMERA TUBE SUPPORT
(INTERCHANGE WITH WHEELCHAIR ARM)

webbing and an adjuster; a Multifit Camera Strap with dual slot fitting clasp and lug fitting D-ring suitable for virtually all SLR cameras; a Contour Strap shaped to minimise slipping over shoulder; a Camera Waist Harness which prevents neck-strap camera swing; a non-slip Shoulder pad for straps up to 25mm wide.

Fig. 22

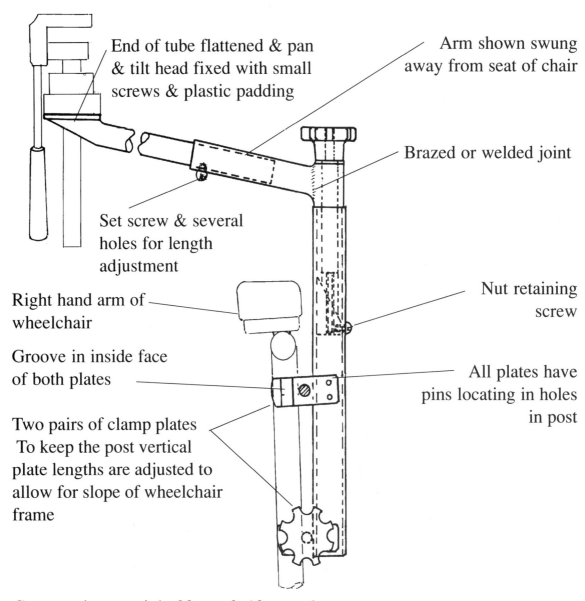

End of tube flattened & pan & tilt head fixed with small screws & plastic padding

Arm shown swung away from seat of chair

Brazed or welded joint

Set screw & several holes for length adjustment

Right hand arm of wheelchair

Nut retaining screw

Groove in inside face of both plates

All plates have pins locating in holes in post

Two pairs of clamp plates To keep the post vertical plate lengths are adjusted to allow for slope of wheelchair frame

Construction - mainly 22mm & 19mm tube & ex-wheelchair knobs

CAMERA MOUNTING FOR WHEELCHAIR
(ESSEX CENTRAL REMAP)

Camera Supports and Clamps for Wheelchair Users
Wheelchair Mounted Camera Support and Equipment Tray (Fig. 21)

The basic idea is a pole piece which fits into the arm-socket on one side of a wheelchair and is then set over at the top to bring the camera it supports to a central position.

The pole can also carry a tray by means of the square flanged adaptor shown; this is optional.

The use of a second pole piece to support the tray from the other side of the chair gives even greater rigidity. (CLIC worked with local school children to make this support.)

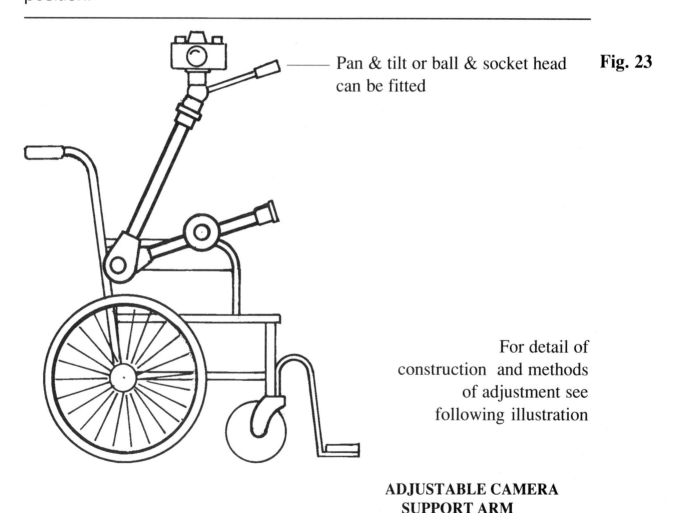

Pan & tilt or ball & socket head can be fitted

Fig. 23

For detail of construction and methods of adjustment see following illustration

ADJUSTABLE CAMERA SUPPORT ARM

Camera Mounting for Wheelchair (Fig.22)

REMAP Essex Central were asked to make a camera support for a photographer using a wheelchair. The support consists of a vertical tube clamped to the arm of the wheelchair from the top of which a horizontal arm is supported.

The arm projects over the wheelchair seat and carries at its end a pan and tilt head. This gives all the usual angular adjustments plus the height adjustment of the central pillar.

Fig. 24

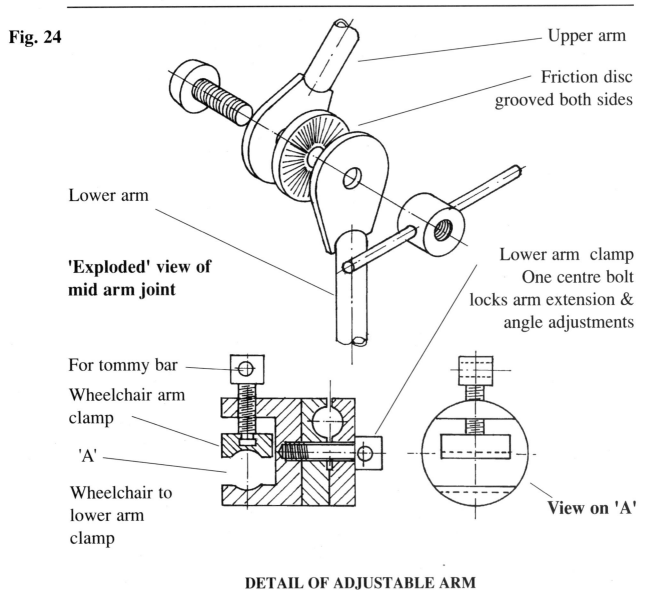

Upper arm

Friction disc
grooved both sides

Lower arm

**'Exploded' view of
mid arm joint**

Lower arm clamp
One centre bolt
locks arm extension &
angle adjustments

For tommy bar

Wheelchair arm
clamp

'A'

Wheelchair to
lower arm
clamp

View on 'A'

DETAIL OF ADJUSTABLE ARM

Fig. 25   **Fig. 26**

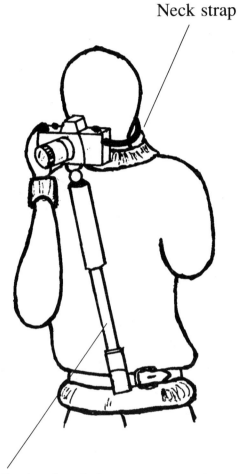

Neck strap

Spring loaded camera support attaching to waist belt

**WAIST BELT
CAMERA SUPPORT**

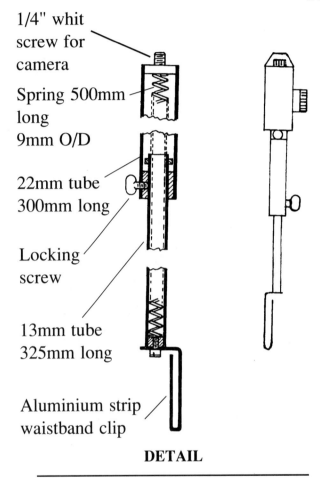

1/4" whit screw for camera

Spring 500mm long 9mm O/D

22mm tube 300mm long

Locking screw

13mm tube 325mm long

Aluminium strip waistband clip

DETAIL

Contained within the vertical tube is an angle-faced nut which, by means of a draw-bolt and the hand wheel at the top of the tube, locks the arm in position when taking a picture, or frees it for positioning at other times.

Some adjustment can be made to the length of the arm by means of the screw and holes provided.

Adjustable Camera Support Arm (Figs 23, 24)
The object of the jointed arm is to provide a camera support

Fig. 27

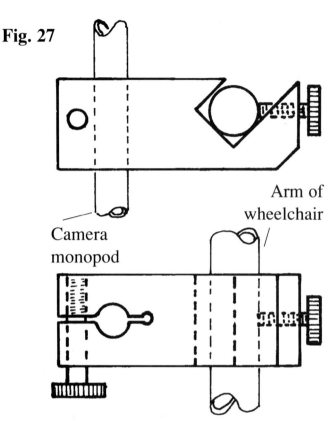

Camera
monopod

Arm of
wheelchair

Clamp made from 36mm
square aluminium bar

CLAMP TO FIX MONOPOD
TO WHEELCHAIR ARM
(BARNET REMAP)

bolts; one locks to the wheelchair, the other locks both the length of extension and the angle of tilt of the lower arm simultaneously. Both lock-bolts are operated by a tommy bar, or length of steel rod which passes through the head of the bolt. The longer the bar the easier it is to turn, (this is a positive advantage).

The top arm carries an adaptor plug, to take either a commercial pan-and-tilt head,

which will clamp to a wheel chair and, with the addition of a pan-and-tilt head or a ball-and-socket joint, will give almost universal position adjustment.

Figs 23, 24 show two arms connected by an adjustable joint and a clamp which secures the lower arm to the wheelchair frame. This clamp has two lock-

Fig. 28

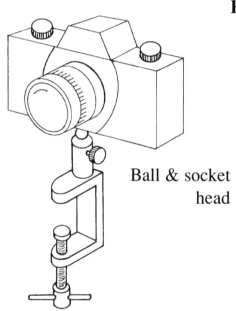

Ball & socket
head

'G' CLAMP CAN BE
FITTED TO BARS, TUBES,
FLAT SURFACES , ETC.

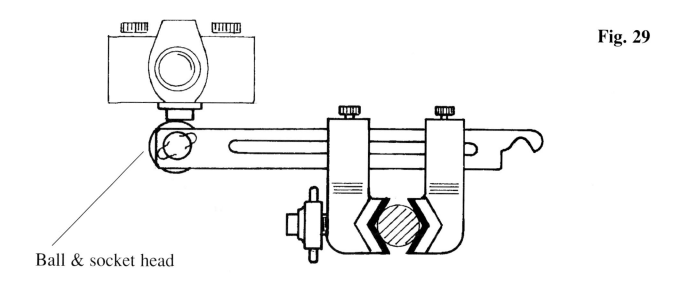

Fig. 29

Ball & socket head

**CULLMANN UNIVERSAL CLAMP WITH PLASTIC
LINED JAWS.**
[MODEL NO. 1004]
(Clamps to tubes, rods, tree branches, tripod legs, etc.)

or a ball-and-socket joint upon which the camera is mounted.

Manufacture of the unit calls for basic engineering operations only: mainly turning, thread tapping and brazing.

*Waist Belt Camera Support
(Figs 25,26)*

Mr J. Burdett, Lincolnshire, has designed a camera support mounted on a waist-belt, for use sitting or standing. This support is spring-loaded to assist lifting the camera. The support attaches to the waist-belt by an aluminium strip bent to fit the belt. [3]

Manfrotto 'Magic Arm'

Manfrotto manufacture a unit called a 'magic arm': a two part 50cm arm with centre locking joint. It has a camera mounting plate at one end and a 'super clamp' can be supplied to attach it to the wheelchair frame. The centre lever locks all ball-and-socket movements; all other joints can be moved independently. It can be used to support the camera in almost any position. Once set in position it is very stable. It requires a firm grip, however, to position the lever and minor alteration of camera position cannot be made without using this lever. Not all wheelchairs have a suitable clamping place, and the clamp itself has a tendency to slip in some positions.

Raise/Lower Camera Support for a Wheelchair

Avery Hill College, Eltham have made a camera support system for a wheelchair user at John Groome's home for the Disabled in Southend. It attaches to the standard range of foldable wheelchairs. Previously, the photographer required another person to accompany him on a trip out. The support made this unnecessary. It has a reversing electric motor which is foot controlled. Operation is effected by an 'on-off-on' switch which causes the assembly to raise, stop and lower according to the wishes of the operator. [4]

Clamp to fix Monopod to Wheelchair Arm (Fig. 27)

Barnet REMAP has devised a clamp to fix to the arm of a wheelchair and hold a monopod for a camera.

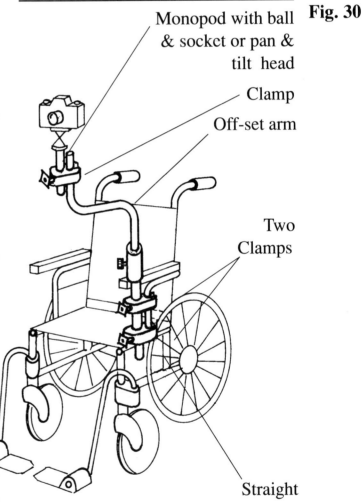

Fig. 30

Monopod with ball & socket or pan & tilt head

Clamp

Off-set arm

Two Clamps

Straight pole

MOBILIA POLE & CLAMP SYSTEM USED TO ATTACH CAMERA TO WHEELCHAIR

Alternative Clamps
(Figs 28, 29, 32)

Ordinary clamps fixed to solid objects are sometimes preferable to using a tripod. With a small ball-and-socket mount most types of lighting or woodwork clamp can be adapted to hold a camera. (Fig. 32).

Nick Burton has this to say on this subject: 'Two more pieces of equipment I have are a hide clamp and a car window clamp, both of which are available

Fig. 32

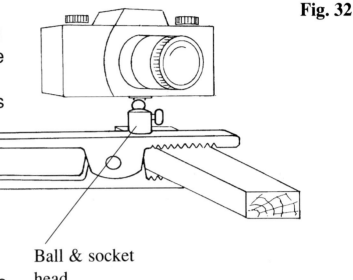

Ball & socket
head

**SPRING GRIP CLAMP HOLDING ON
TIMBER BATTEN**

 Fig. 31

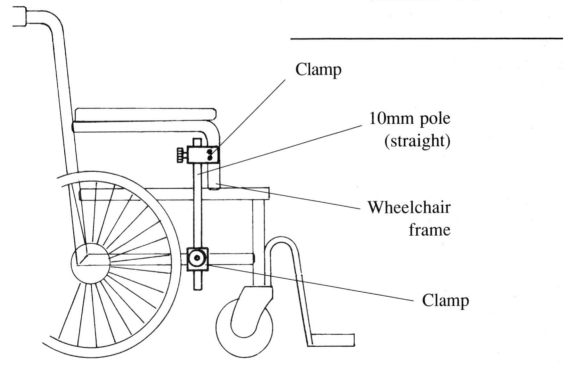

Clamp

10mm pole
(straight)

Wheelchair
frame

Clamp

**MOBILIA METHOD OF HOLDING 10MM - STRAIGHT POLE
RIGIDLY WITH TWO ADAPTORS**

from shops specialising in bird watching accessories and photography shops, (addresses of suppliers can be obtained from bird watching magazines), although I had my hide clamp made by a friend.

The hide clamp, (Fig. 28), is a 'G' shaped device which fixes to a shelf, ledge or similar such place in a bird watching hide. Cameras, telescopes, etc., can then be fitted on a tripod head on top of a pole which slides into the clamp itself. The car window clamp simply screws onto a half-opened car window and then cameras, telescopes, etc., are

WHEELCHAIR CLAMPS & ADAPTORS SYSTEM

Fig. 33

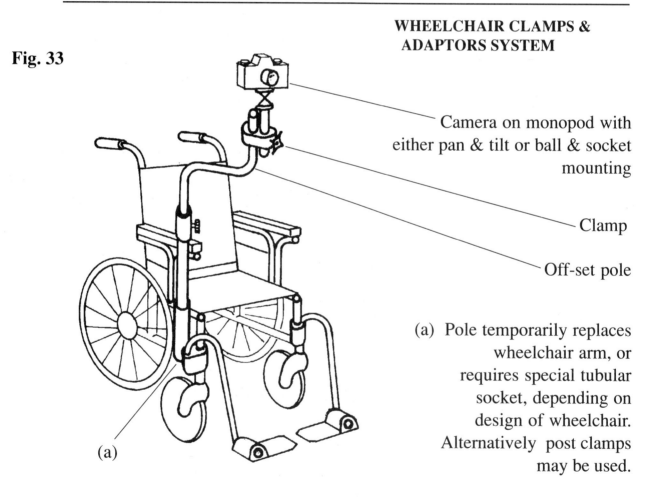

Camera on monopod with either pan & tilt or ball & socket mounting

Clamp

Off-set pole

(a) Pole temporarily replaces wheelchair arm, or requires special tubular socket, depending on design of wheelchair. Alternatively post clamps may be used.

(a)

POLES AND ADAPTORS BY MOBILIA
(Formerly Orange Aids)

held on by means of a screw into their tripod fixings.'

Cullmann Universal Clamp (Fig.29)
Cullmann make a universal clamp which it is claimed fits on rods, tables, tree boughs, etc.

Mobilia
(Figs 30, 31, 33)
6 Crown Street Mews,
St Ives, Huntingdon,
Cambs. PE17 4EB
Tel: 0480 492022

Mobilia, (formerly 'Orange Aids'), makes a complete system of mobility aids for disabled people. According to a 1987 DHSS Field Study, Mobilia products provide an 'immediate solution to many problems where previous attempts have proved unsuccessful'.

Mobilia is a system for attaching cameras, binoculars, trays and other working surfaces to DHSS and private wheelchairs.

The components of the system are a wide range of clamps,

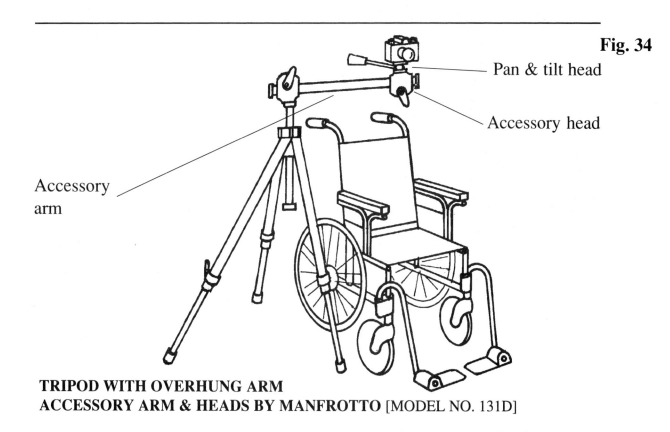

Fig. 34

Pan & tilt head

Accessory head

Accessory arm

TRIPOD WITH OVERHUNG ARM
ACCESSORY ARM & HEADS BY MANFROTTO [MODEL NO. 131D]

adaptors, poles, connectors, radius arms. In fact, the basic requirements for attaching and positioning aids where required and providing a variable angle worksurface. The system enables cameras of all types to be attached to most DHSS and other wheelchairs.

Figs 30,31,33 are examples of the Mobilia range.

In order to simplify the selection and ordering of equipment, Mobilia will shortly be selling their most requested applications, (e.g. a wheelchair camera mounting), as pre-packaged sets.

Mobilia is about to market an A Frame, (including ball and socket fitting for cameras, etc.,).

The frame can be used where arm fatigue is a problem, for example, using a 35mm camera with telephoto lens. The frame comprises a camera stand with neck harness. A second neck strap should be used for the camera. The A Frame has telescopic legs.

Mobilia also stock a camera pan &tilt kit, and a Disc/Instamatic camera kit.

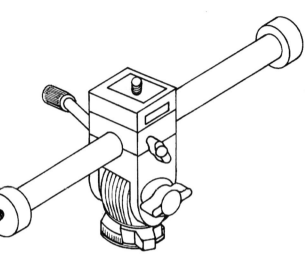

Fig. 35

RAIL CARRYING HEAD
[CULLMANN MACRO RAIL
HEAD MODEL 962]

Overhung Arm
(Figs.34, 35)

As an alternative to fixing the camera on the wheelchair by a system of poles and adaptors, the camera can be supported on a tripod and made accessible from a wheelchair by the use of an overhung arm. Fig.34 shows the 'Manfrotto' type of fitting and Fig.35, the Cullmann Accessory Rail with Supporting Head.

CHAPTER SEVEN : AUXILIARY AIDS

The following is a short list of aids which may have an application in taking photographs or in using the darkroom. They are available from Homecraft by mail-order.

(i)   portable aluminium wheelchair ramp, adjustable in width and folds in half for easy transport. It has non-slip pads on the underside, and a gripping cover along the length of each track.

(ii)   extended tongs which have a soft gripping jaw with magnet.

(ii)   tubing in polythene which makes a soft built up handgrip supplied in meter lengths of varying diameters.

(iv) a grip-kit. This is a two part epoxy compound which, when mixed together, is like plasticine. It can be moulded to all shapes and will stick to any surface.

(v) dycem is a plastic material which has a gripping surface on both sides. It is non-slip. Dycem must be kept clean to maintain its properties. It can be bought in rolls.

Homecraft Supplies Ltd,
Lower Moor Estate,
Kirkby-in-Ashfield
Nottingham. N917 7JZ
Tel: 0623 754047

Showroom, London.
Chester Care,
16 Englands Lane
London. NW3 4TC
Tel: 071 586 2166

CHAPTER EIGHT : ACCESS

New Buildings

The Disabled Persons' Act, 1981, imposes a duty on planning authorities to draw the attention of persons to whom they grant planning permission to certain statutory and other provisions relating to access for disabled people to buildings and other premises used by the public. For further advice contact:

Access Committee for England, Centre on Environment for the Handicapped, 35 Great Smith St, London. SW1P 3BJ Tel: 071 222 7980

Community Organisations

(For a list of Community Organisations with which we have had contact, see Chapter 2, pp.24-28.)

In correspondence with community organisations, it was found that many workers were 'apologetic' for not having 'given more thought' to access and/or making facilities accessible. Inevitably, however, responsibility was always referred away to lack of resources. In fact, the real barrier would seem to be not resources, but how those resources are allocated.

There was the community darkroom that went to the expense of moving its darkroom from inaccessible attic to inaccessible basement. There was the photographic society that installed a lift to make its first floor darkroom accessible, but didn't adapt worktops, sinks or equipment. There was the Media Centre which made 'major alterations' to its darkroom floor level to make possible some photography workshops for disabled people. This was later stripped out because the alterations made it 'unsuitable' for able-bodied use.

Photography Courses in Further Education

Lack of access means segregated arrangements or exclusion. Again the barrier is not resource or movement, but attitude.

Access can seriously affect the chance of an applicant 'getting a place' at an Art School or College of Further Education to do photography or any other course.

One senior lecturer justified the admission of only six disabled students in as many years by stating: 'there are no lifts, disabled students cannot negotiate the stairways - especially when carrying work.'

Why should a prospective student be excluded from a course because nobody is prepared to carry his/her work?

Is not admission on merit the correct criterion when interviewing an applicant, whether disabled or not?

The head of an art school commenting on a survey carried out at the school on the practicability of admitting a wheelchair user to a course, wrote: 'What I am very conscious of is, not only the problem of movement....but the physical and emotional stress that the responsibility for "being responsible" for assisting a disabled student can bring.' The applicant was not admitted. [1]

Fig. 36

'WELL, THIS CERTAINLY PUTS AN END TO OUR PLANS TO CONQUER THE UNIVERSE.'

Approach to and Inside Buildings

The following recommendations are included in 1979 British Standard Code of Practice Access for Disabled People to Buildings, (BS5810). Access Data Sheets are available from RADAR.

Dropped Kerbs

In places where movement has to be made from roadway to pavements, the surfaces concerned should merge. The resulting gradient should not exceed 1:10.

Level or Ramped Approach

The width of the approach route should be not less that 1200mm. Where the approach is ramped the gradient should not exceed 1:12. Where the gradient exceeds 1:5, a handrail should be provided to each side of the ramp.

Stepped Approach

Goings should be not less than 280mm, and should be uniform.

Risers should be not higher than 150mm, and should be uniform.

The vertical rise of any flight should not exceed 1200mm. A handrail should be provided to each side of the steps or centrally.

Entrance doors

Should give a clear opening width of not less than 800mm.

Internal doors

Accessible areas should give a clear opening width of not less than 750mm.

Internal Staircases

A handrail should be provided to each side of the stair.

WC Compartment

Doors should open outwards or slide.

The doors should be operable from outside in the event of an emergency.

Support rails should be provided.

A rinse basin should be provided where practicable, in a position where it can be used by a person seated on the W.C.

The rim of the W.C. bowl should be a minimum height of 400mm above floor level, with the seat approx. 450mm above floor level, to facilitate transfer from wheelchair.

CHAPTER NINE : STUDIO WORK

Home Studio

The aim with a temporary studio is to make the least possible disturbance to furniture, pressing into service whatever is convenient. For portrait or still-life photography, it will often be possible to use natural light from a window balanced by a reflector. If there is insufficient natural light, flash can be added.

There are many articles of furniture in the home that can be used for mounting lights at an accessible level. Grip clamps should be padded with felt. If you are using powerful lamps you should be careful not to overload the circuit.

Photo-light stands are usually made with aluminium alloy and are very light. They can be floor standing or mounted by clamp on, say, the back of a chair. It is important to keep the floor as clear as possible for maximum access. To facilitate this, reflectors can be mounted on a light tubular frame so that they can be propped or hung at any angle.

You will find in the home many of the things you need: cloth, backdrops, board or card for shaders, a desk lamp to act as a flood in still life, kitchen foil to use as reflectors, etc.

Fig. 37

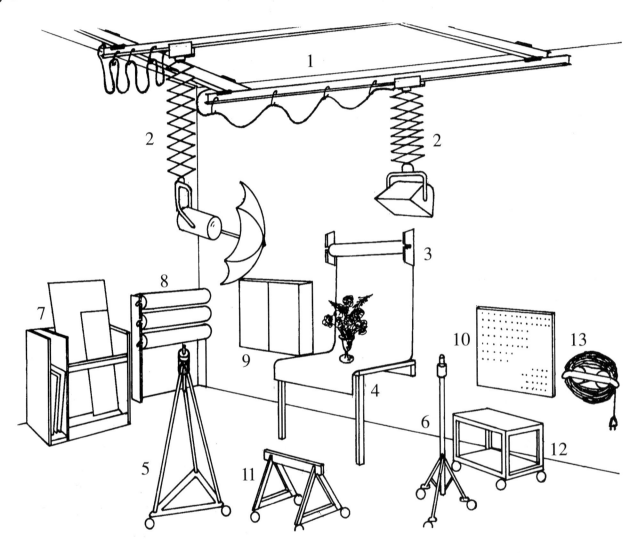

STUDIO EQUIPMENT AND FITTINGS

KEY LIST FIG. 37 STUDIO EQUIPMENT AND FITTINGS

1 Overhead track to keep light fittings off the floor
2 Pantograph supports enable lights to be raised out of way when not in use
3 Brackets for rolls of background material when in use
4 Hinged table lies flat against wall when not in use
5 Camera tripod on trolley with castors
6 Light fittings stand on castors
7 Rack for storage of flat reflector or background sheets
8 Rack for storage of rolls of coloured backgrounds
9 Cupboard for small items
10 Peg-board for hanging tools
11 Trestle on castors for general use
12 General purpose rolling trolley
13 Storage rack for long electric cables

Community Studio
Equipment & Fittings

Fig. 37 does not attempt to show a studio set up for action, but rather some of the fittings and equipment to be found there. The key list makes this drawing self-explanatory.

A studio for wheelchair users must have open access. A studio floor can quickly become covered with photo-lights, leads, backdrops, etc.

Hinged work surfaces, wall brackets and boxed frames to prevent properties from sliding to the floor will help to create space. Background rolls should be mounted on the wall, and not between posts. Where possible, all equipment should be mounted on castors to facilitate clearance. A trolley may be used, amongst other things, as a surface for still life. Doors should be sliding or swing.

Lights

In Fig. 37, the lights are shown suspended at high level, by pantograph, from a track. This raises the question of accessibility when raised.

Basic studio lighting usually consists of one light at high level on one side of the subject, a second at mid-point on the other, and a third as spot or background, at low level. Other lights can be added as subject or effects increase in complexity.

With accessibility of lights in mind, cost, and the need to keep the floor area clear for using a wheelchair, a scheme for a community studio was devised. (Figs. 39-43).

The primary requirement was that all lighting should be mounted from the ceiling or from the wall. At the same time it was necessary to ensure that lamp positioning could be adjusted by someone using a wheelchair.

Fig. 38 shows a ceiling light, pantograph mounted, attached to a ceiling track, which runs from one end of the ceiling to the other. A pantograph allows a light to be pulled up and down, as well as along. Use of a pantograph by

Fig. 38

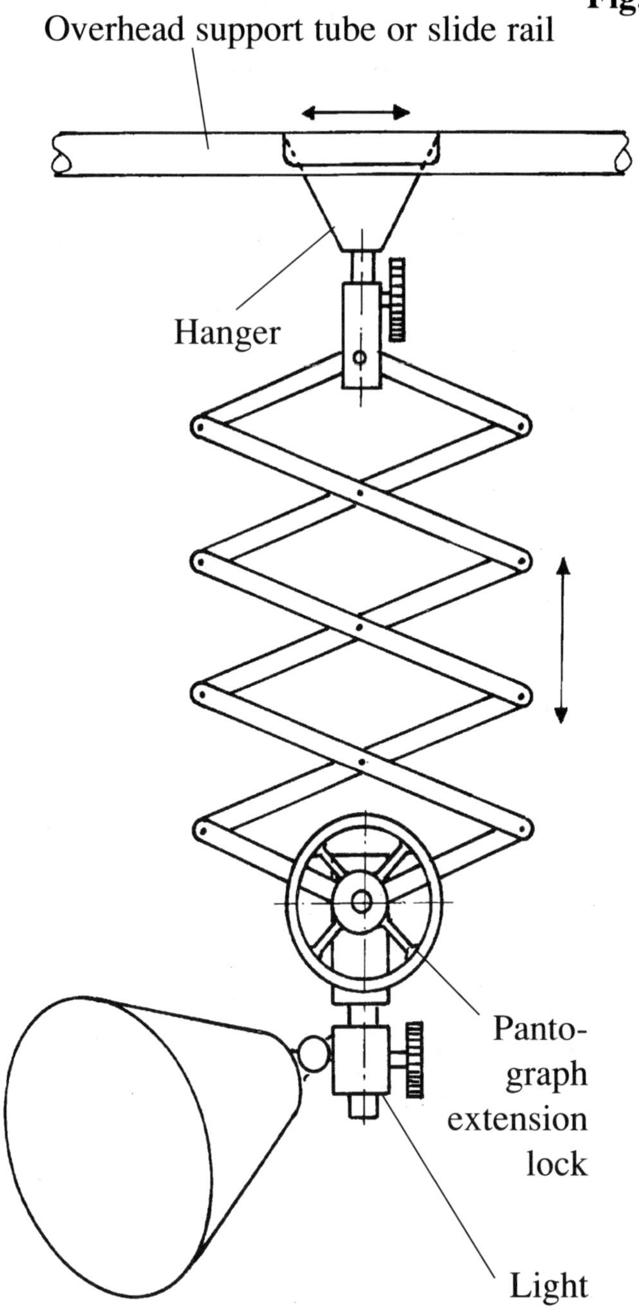

Overhead support tube or slide rail

Hanger

Panto-graph extension lock

Light fitting & clamp

**PANTOGRAPH TYPE
STUDIO LIGHT SUPPORT**

a wheelchair user would normally require a facilitator. Pantographs and ceiling track could be

motorised, but only very expensively. It may be supposed that a cranking rod would facilitate

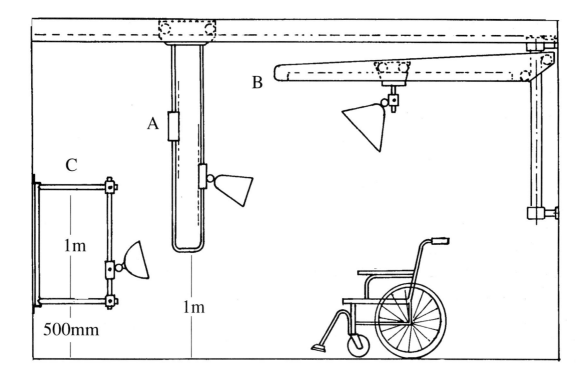

Fig. 39

Light A (Fig. 41) can traverse the length of ceiling beam and height adjusted over length of trackway tube

Light B (Fig. 42) horizontal traverse to cantilever beam length & vertical adjustment to height of support column

Light C (Fig. 43) can be set from 500mm to 1500mm from ground level and pivot about rear post

Note:

(1) All light position adjustments can be made from wheelchair - see sketch for suggested heights

(2) Light B is motorised and controlled from portable electric box

**COMMUNITY PROJECT SUSPENDED LIGHTING LEAVING STUDIO
FLOOR CLEAR**

Fig. 40

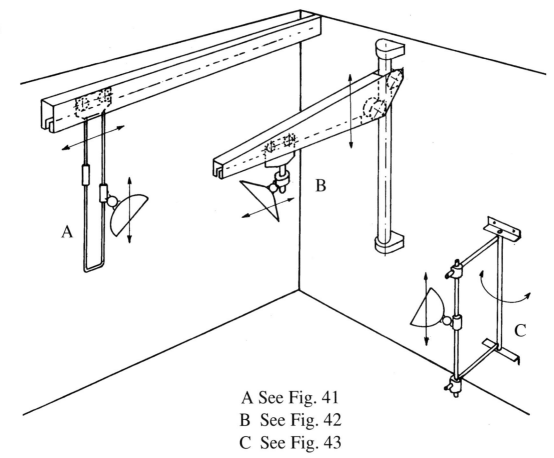

A See Fig. 41
B See Fig. 42
C See Fig. 43

**DIAGRAMATIC OF 'CLEAR FLOOR'
STUDIO LIGHTING**

operation from wheelchair level. The difficulty here is that a cranking rod requires a firm base from which to operate the handle, as in the case of the old high level school window. The handle, in turn, may be difficult to operate. The idea of pantograph lighting is, however, that it should float. It has no firm anchorage to which to fit a winding handle. You cannot bracket it to anything.

The designs in Figs. 41-43 attempt to overcome such problems.

Fig. 41

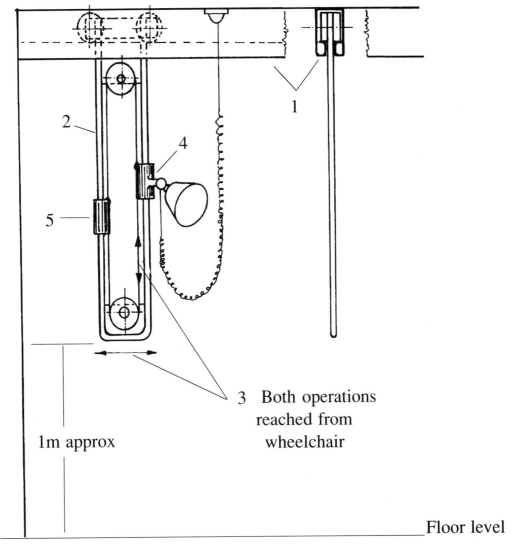

1m approx

3 Both operations
reached from
wheelchair

Floor level

1 Folded aluminium channel section fixed to ceiling
2 Aluminium tube frame suspended from wheeled trolley running in
channel section
3 Endless cord for raising and lowering light fitting
4 Light fitting sliding on aluminium tube and fixed to endless cord
5 Weight to counter-balance light fitting - this slides on aluminium tube
& fixed to endless cord

**COMMUNITY PROJECT CEILING
MOUNTED LIGHTING LEAVING FLOOR
AREA CLEAR (LIGHT A)**

Fig. 42

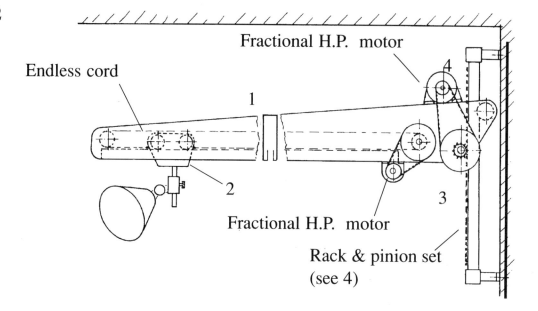

1 Folded aluminium cantilever arm with integral trolley track
2 Trolley carrying light fitting
3 Lateral positioning of trolley - fractional horse power reversing motor with toothed belt drive
4 Raising & lowering of arm - fractional horse power motor (reversing) with toothed belt drive to a rack & pinion set on support column

**COMMUNITY PROJECT MOTORISED HIGH LEVEL
LIGHT MOUNTED ON WALL (LIGHT B)**

Fig. 41 shows a ceiling mounted lighting arrangement with an endless cord for raising and lowering the light fitting.

Fig. 42 shows a motorised high-level light mounted on the wall with trolley track and reversing motor with belt-drive.

Fig. 43 shows a 'slip-in' low-level wall mounting for a studio lamp. The lamp position is adjusted:

(i)   by raising or lowering the clamp

(ii) by pivoting the frame.

Fig. 43

1 Two horizontal & one vertical tube welded together or clamped
2 Post carrying light fitting clamped to top & bottom tube
3 Angle iron sections along studio walls

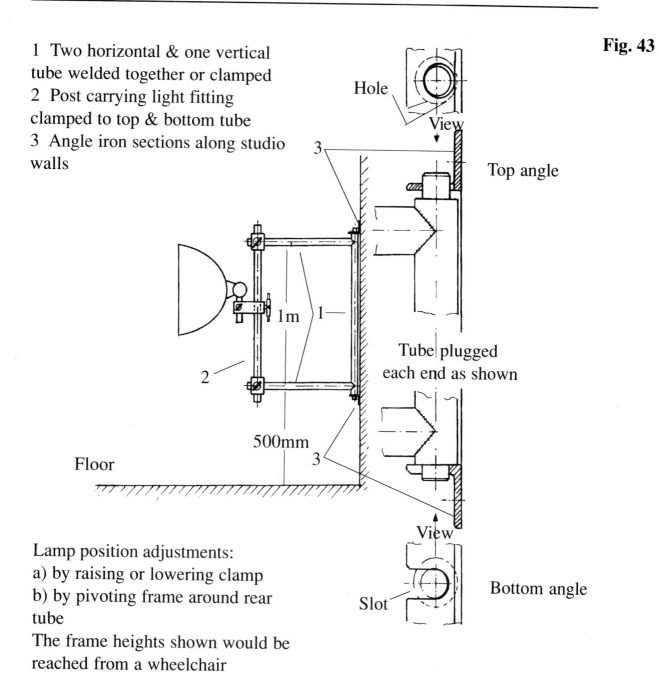

Lamp position adjustments:
a) by raising or lowering clamp
b) by pivoting frame around rear tube
The frame heights shown would be reached from a wheelchair

**SLIP-IN LOW-LEVEL WALL MOUNTING
FOR STUDIO LAMP (LIGHT C)**

CHAPTER TEN : THE DARKROOM

Printing and processing need not take up much room. Indeed, to process film you do not even need a darkroom. A light-tight changing bag and a daylight processing tank are all that is necessary. Using the bag and threading the film take practice, but it is the same process as in the darkroom.

DARKROOM LAYOUT

Fig. 44

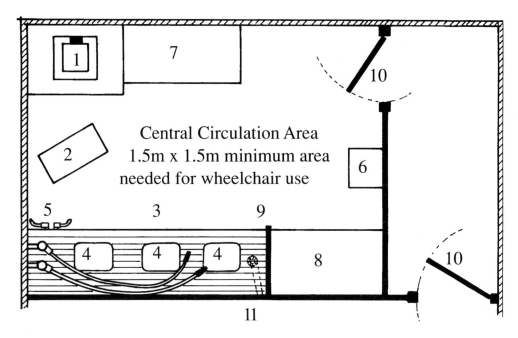

Central Circulation Area
1.5m x 1.5m minimum area
needed for wheelchair use

1 Enlarger
2 Movable surface, (trolley)
3 Slatted sink plumbed to waste - installed at wheelchair level
4 Process trays
5 Taps with swiller tubes & extended handles at front of bench

6 Dryer cabinet
7 Work bench (See Figs. 47-48)
8 Work bench and space for possible second enlarger
9 Partition between wet and dry areas
10 Swing doors
11 Drain

In order to determine layout, It will be helpful to visualise the kind of movements you will need to make in the darkroom. Will it be possible to move backwards and forwards across the darkroom? Will a central circulation area be necessary? Black and white printing, for example, because of open tray processing, requires more space than colour printing. The darkroom should be so arranged that you can move in a logical progression round it. (Fig. 44).

Let us consider in outline home and adapted darkroom.

Home Darkroom

The advantage of your own darkroom is that you can do your own printing and you have control in the composition of the image. Moreover, having prints enlarged by a laboratory is often an expensive business.

Running water is not essential to a darkroom. You must use water where you find it. The trouble with a cupboard darkroom without a sink is risk of spillage. It will be necessary to take the wet prints outside to dry. In many cases such an arrangement may be unworkable as you may not be in a position to carry water to and from the darkroom.

In the home darkroom, as in any darkroom, the basic principle of darkroom layout - the separation of wet and dry areas - *must* be observed.

For reasons of hygiene, the kitchen is not a suitable place to have a darkroom. Chemicals should not be stored there. The obvious choice is the bathroom, since it has a constant supply of running water. Quite often, a bathroom does not have windows to black out. If you do need to black out windows, then they may be sealed very cheaply by using a double lining of black disposable bags. You can use fitted board to convert the bath to a bench which may be hinged to the wall and held flush against the wall when bathing. (Fig. 45).

It is important to keep the wet and dry areas as separate as possible. If it is not possible to stand the enlarger away from the bath bench, then ensure that it is raised above the processing dishes. This may mean using a high stool. You should use cord-operated switches, earth all electrical equipment and fuse plugs at their correct amperage.

Fig. 45

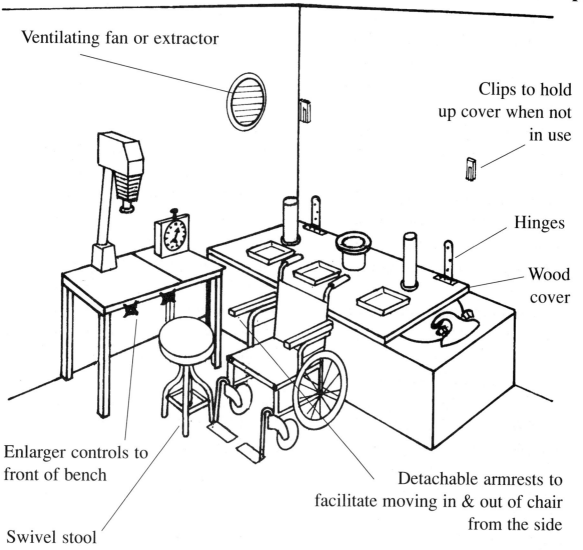

Ventilating fan or extractor

Clips to hold
up cover when not
in use

Hinges

Wood
cover

Enlarger controls to
front of bench

Detachable armrests to
facilitate moving in & out of chair
from the side

Swivel stool

BATHROOM/DARKROOM

Avoid extension cables and boxes that can be tripped over.

In colour printing, the use of a light-tight drum for maintaining high temperatures and ready mixed chemicals means that you need work in the dark with the door closed for only a few minutes. After that you can leave the door open. In most cases this will give adequate ventilation. If, however, you are processing black and white prints over open dishes with rising vapours, some ventilation will be necessary. However, to install an extractor or air vent may not always be practical.

Adapted Community Darkroom
(Figs 46, 47, 48)

Since the primary concern of this book is design in so far as it touches on photographic equipment and/or adaption of equipment, (see Chapter One), it is not within its ambit to consider the many detailed problems of adapted darkroom layout and its furnishing and fittings. The following list only scratches the surface of such detail:

(i)   physical and visual access to sinks and developing tanks

(ii)   accessibility of wall-switches

(iii) adapted sockets

(iv) working surfaces which can be moved to increase circulation area, e.g., by use of slotted brackets, or which can be hooked up against a wall, etc.

(v)   movable worktops such as a trolley or an inset rotating worktop

(vi) taps with extended arms and/ or which can be operated at front of sink

(vii) extra large skirting board to protect plaster work at low-level

(viii) low-level heating

(ix) worktops should be so constructed that a person using a wheelchair can run their wheelchair under the bench to allow both access to shelving and work close up to equipment. [1]

For example, as a solution in (ix), because there is restricted reach from a seated position, a bench designed in a semi-circular bank shape would allow apparatus to be reached from a centrally seated position. (Figs 49-51).

Fig. 46

Slotted brackets for adjustable height shelving

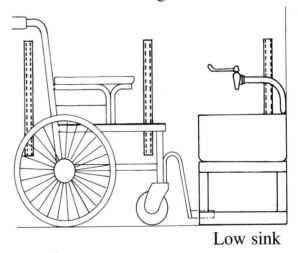

Low sink

EASY ACCESS SINK AND SHELVING

BENCHES

Fig. 47

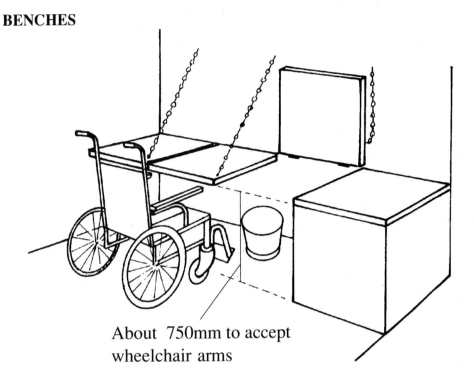

About 750mm to accept
wheelchair arms

SINKS

Fig. 48

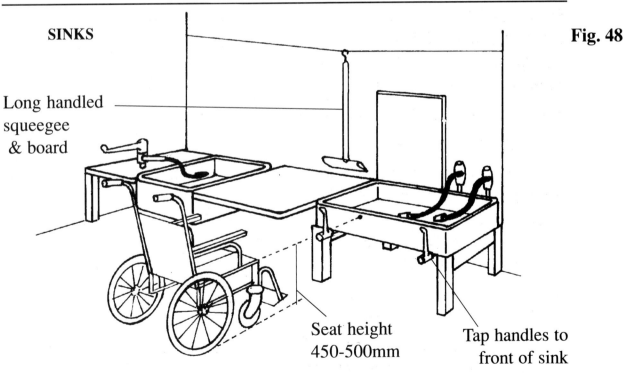

Long handled
squeegee
& board

Seat height
450-500mm

Tap handles to
front of sink

Fig. 49

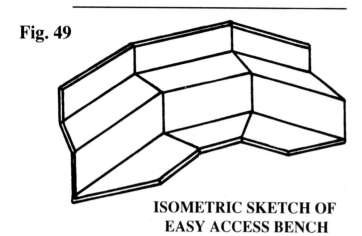

**ISOMETRIC SKETCH OF
EASY ACCESS BENCH**

The entrance to the darkroom should have doors that slide or swing. On entering, a light-block area will stop unexpected light from being cast internally.

Fig. 50

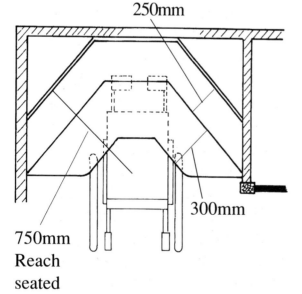

250mm

750mm
Reach
seated

300mm

**BENCH SHOWN FITTED INTO
1500 X 750MM ALCOVE**

Fig. 51

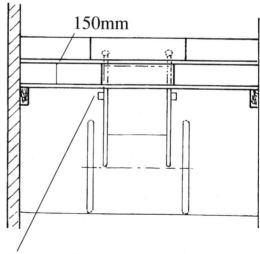

150mm

Bench height
to clear
wheelchair
arms

EASY ACCESS BENCH

CHAPTER ELEVEN : DARKROOM EQUIPMENT

Enlargers

An enlarger is a projection printer similar to a slide projector, usually mounted vertically. It has three controls:

(i)   size

(ii)   focus

(iii)   aperture

Today, you can find enlargers with motorised movement of lens and complete control from baseboard. Attached to the baseboard will be a control box which incorporates a timer, blower and focusing controls, together with scale, light, illumination and exposure auto-button. Such enlargers would be ideal for disabled photograpers, but are made for commercial, not disability photography. (See De Vere 1085, 108A/M).

Roll-paper easels are available for horizontal projection. This allows work on a flatter, more accessible level. (Fig. 37).

The size control on an enlarger is normally operated from the right hand side. Fujimoto, however, make an enlarger with left hand up and down control, (Fujimoto G70 Computer). It has a twin illumination system. Focusing control on all Fujimoto enlargers is on the right hand side. [1]

REMAP Barnet has modified an enlarger for left hand use. The spindles of the existing adjustment controls were extended through the left hand side and large knobs fixed to the spindles. (Fig.52).

When choosing an enlarger it is important to check the head controls for accessibility. Their position varies from enlarger to enlarger. For example, on the Fujimoto 450M-C, the hand controls are positioned on the head carriage; on the DV 504 DVW, which is a wall mounted enlarger, they are positioned at back of base; on the DV504 DVB, which is bench standing, and the DV 504DVFD, which is floor standing, they are positioned at front of base. Controls on the head carriage or at the back of the baseboard may be inaccessible.

It may be possible to mount a bench standing enlarger so that all its parts are accessible for someone using a wheelchair.

The enlarger would be carried on a counter-balanced table giving a 600mm-900mm lift. (Fig. 53). This would allow all working parts, from baseboard to lamphouse, to be presented to the operator at his/her level of choice. If, in addition, the centre of the table were in the form of a turntable, not only would all controls be at table level, but all controls could be turned to the front.

Nothing elaborate would be required. The lift would be based on the tried and proven window-sash principle. So mounted, any additional modification to the enlarger required by the user would be simple to implement. If the enlarger were positioned in this way each operation, except focusing, could be carried out at table level.

The baseboard and the enlarger should be so balanced that the work required to raise and

Fig. 52

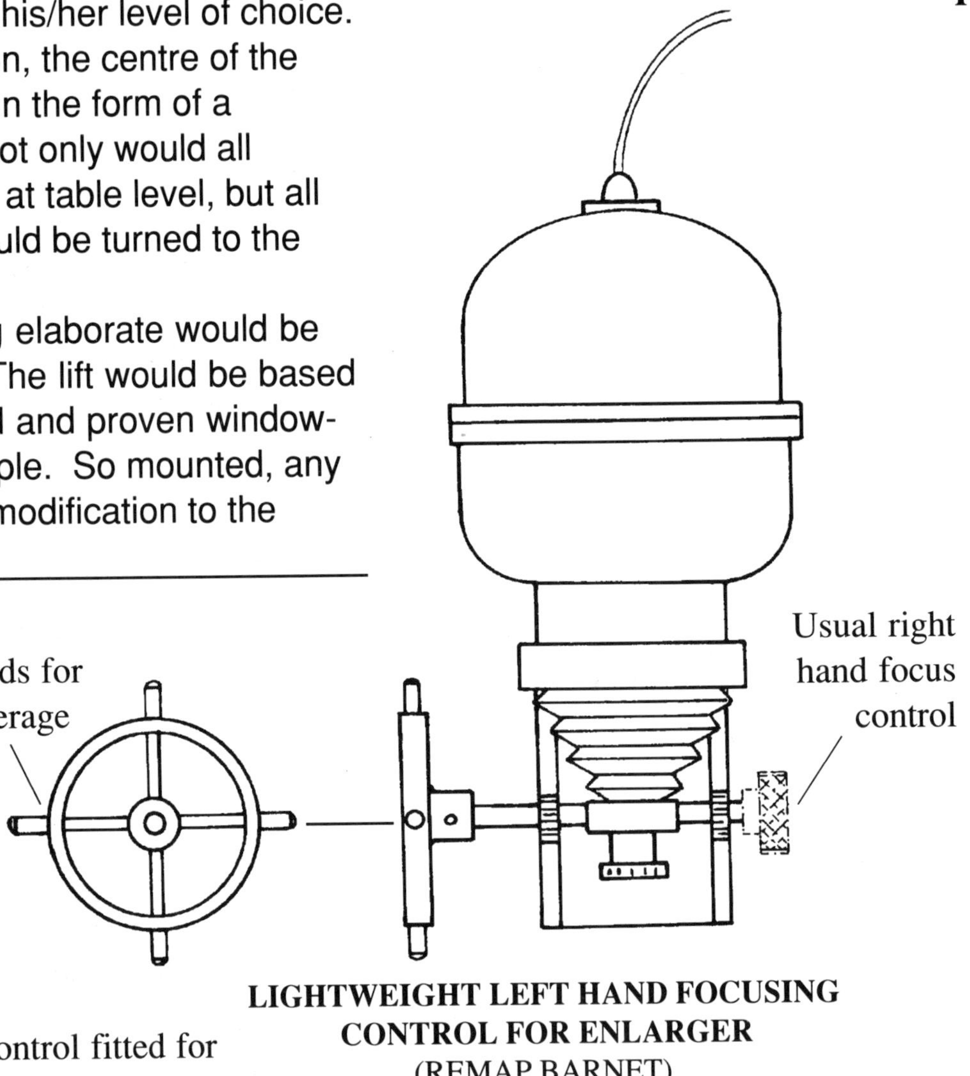

External rods for greater leverage

Usual right hand focus control

Enlarged control fitted for left hand use

LIGHTWEIGHT LEFT HAND FOCUSING CONTROL FOR ENLARGER
(REMAP BARNET)

**VARIABLE HEIGHT & ROTATING
ENLARGER TABLE**

Fig. 53

(Table shown at
highest
position)

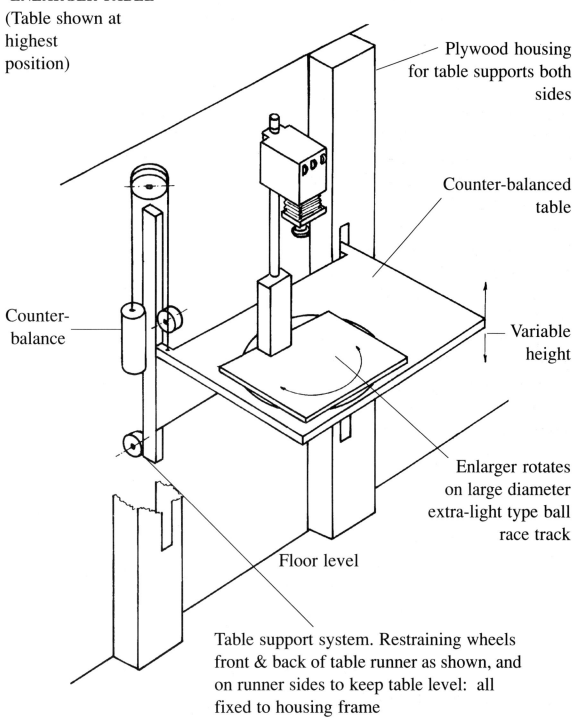

Plywood housing
for table supports both
sides

Counter-balanced
table

Counter-
balance

Variable
height

Enlarger rotates
on large diameter
extra-light type ball
race track

Floor level

Table support system. Restraining wheels
front & back of table runner as shown, and
on runner sides to keep table level: all
fixed to housing frame

lower the board is that necessary to overcome inertia and friction only. For this reason all working parts should be ball-race mounted.

If possible, the enlarger should be autofocus. Otherwise, extended or motorised focus controls will be necessary.

Motorised Enlargers

A motorised enlarger will enable the head to be adjusted at baseboard level. Most controls consist of a knob on a spindle. This arrangement is ideal for conversion to motor drive. It is a simple matter to replace the enlarger control knob with an electric motor.

The motor will have to do work varying from raising the enlarger lamp or head, to the relatively delicate operation of focusing the lens. Most electric motors run at the speed of several thousands of revolutions per minute. It will therefore be necessary to connect the motor to the enlarger control spindle by means of a speed reduction gearbox. This will reduce the number of revolutions of the motor to a suitable working speed.

If a motor of variable speed type is used, a flexible control, giving fast run-up speed and accurate final positioning is provided.

Where a control which does not require continuous rotary motion, such as the 'click-stop' iris of a lens, is to be power operated, a push-pull arm can be clamped to the 'click-stop' ring, and operated by an electric solenoid. (See p.8, Cost.)

Light

Enlargers have two kinds of illumination. The condenser enlarger gives a sharp light source which makes focusing easier. The diffused or soft focus head uses an opal sheet to diffuse light. Consequently it is more difficult to focus in its dull, blue light.

Fig. 54

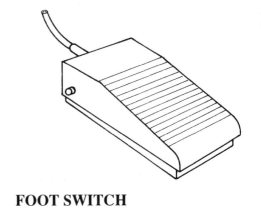

FOOT SWITCH

Fig. 55

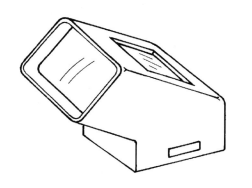

**SCREEN TYPE FOCUSING
MAGNIFIER**

signal once every second. On some models a buzzer indicates the end of the timed interval. (Fig. 56).

A digital timer may enable use with restricted arm movement.

Focus

To set focus, it is helpful to use a focus magnifier. This may require sitting on a high stool. CLIC recommend a Durst focus magnifier for angled viewing like a mini TV screen. (Fig.55).

Footswitch

A footswitch may be used to operate the enlarger timer. You can connect most models to the exposure timer, or directly to the enlarger. (Fig. 54).

Timers

A luminous dial and pointer helps to see in dim safelight conditions.

Alternatively, you can use an audible timer. It makes a sound

Fig. 56

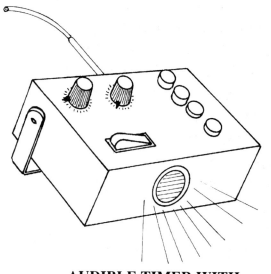

**AUDIBLE TIMER WITH
FREQUENCY VOLUME CONTROLS
ETC.**

CHAPTER TWELVE : PROCESSING SOLUTIONS

You should always ask a manufacturer of processing solutions for a hazard data sheet. Most constituents of processing chemicals are not considered hazardous, but some are when inhaled. Over-exposure to certain chemicals, especially developer, can irritate the eyes and the respiratory system. Splashes entering the eye can cause discomfort and damage. Prolonged or repeated contact with the skin may lead to skin irritation or even dermatitis and may aggravate asthma.

It is important to avoid close inhalation of vapours. A wheelchair user or a person working from a stool is particularly susceptible to noxious chemicals in the darkroom. It may be advisable to wear a mask and gloves and even eye protection. Stopbath is certainly most unpleasant, and, although it does have the benefit of prolonging the active life of fixer, water can be used instead, (provided you are using resin-coated paper as opposed to fibre based papers).

Generally, in reducing chemical pollution, there must be advantages in using liquid processing rather than chemical powders which have to be made up.

If chemicals are splashed in the eyes, they should be rinsed out immediately with tepid water and medical advice sought. Spilt chemicals should be cleaned up as soon as possible.

Powder chemicals and the residue from dried solutions may become airborn and inhaled. Do not mix different types of processing solution. Addition of developer to fixer can lead to the formation of ammonia vapour.

Anyone with poor or low resistance is particularly at risk when using a darkroom. Ventilation should be the first consideration when constructing a darkroom, yet it is very often the last. Photography magazines do not mention the hazards at all. They talk about experiments with processing but do not mention the danger of the chemicals, especially concentrates.

People are often eager to cut corners on ventilation costs and there is widely differing advice on whether it is necessary.

The Drager Device: the air in a darkroom can be tested for chemicals by use of Drager Tubes. These are glass tubes with gas-typical reagents. Unfortunately the sampling tubes have to be evaluated in a laboratory. The tubes can be used for measuring personal exposure in the breathing zone and for air investigation in the confined space of the darkroom. On the spot detection of pollutants is made possible by use of the Drager Tube and a pump by means of which the sampling air is drawn through the tubes. Pollutants are indicated amongst other methods by discolouration of the tubes. [1]

CHAPTER THIRTEEN : FILM PROCESSING

Film Loading

Film should be handled by its edges. It is difficult not to bend, mark, or kink it. Some people may prefer to have the laboratory process the film and to print from a negative which has not been subject to these risks.

There are two types of developing tank and reel: plastic and stainless steel. A plastic reel has the advantage that it is loaded by edge feeding the film. Once you have threaded the two lugs at the entry slot you have only to feed the film an inch or so with your hands before you wind the film, by rotating one edge and then the other. To load film onto a steel reel requires continuous hand contact with the film, bowing the film all the time, until it is loaded.

The solution in a plastic tank can be agitated by using an agitator rod, whereas the heavier stainless steel tank must be agitated, during processing, by turning the tank upside down at regular intervals.

Developing Tank Loading Aid
(Fig. 57)

REMAP Great Yarmouth and Lowestoft has devised a method of threading film on to a tank reel, using one hand. Mount film spool, (remove from cassette), onto the adaptor and stand on

Fig. 57

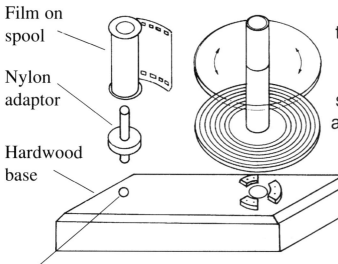

Film on spool

Nylon adaptor

Hardwood base

Hole to accept developing tank scroll boss

DEVELOPING TANK SCROLL LOADING AID
(REMAP GREAT YARMOUTH & LOWESTOFT)

base, (there is a small hole in the hardwood base to accept this). Locate developing tank reel or scroll in large hole shown in the drawing, and feed the film from spool to scroll. Practice is needed for this operation, but it can be performed with one hand. (Fig. 57).

Fixed Bench Loader

In theory, a fixed bench loader with handle and film guide means steady manipulation of film being wound in, thereby avoiding scratches, fingermarks etc. The film is guided evenly at the outer edges of the perforation while being loaded onto the reel.

In practice, members of CLIC have not found the fixed bench loader to be very helpful.

Film Drying

Perhaps the cheapest method of drying film is to hang the film by clips, or by a clothes-hanger, and to blow-dry with a hairdryer. (Fig. 58). [1]

Most drying cabinets are made of metal and have a heater in the top or base, a fan to circulate the heat and a dust-filter. These are expensive. The cheapest types have a plastic

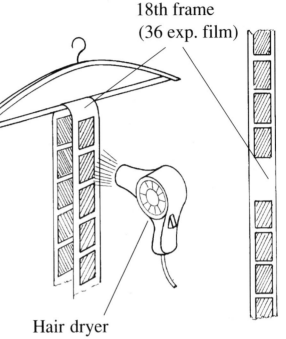

Fig. 58

18th frame
(36 exp. film)

Hair dryer

FILM DRYING

sleeve which is draped from the heating head. Because of the height of the cabinet, necessary to accommodate the length of the film, the hanging rail may be inaccessible to someone using a wheelchair. Table-top models are available, but do not accommodate very long strips of film.

Washing tanks and dryers are available in one complete system. The film washing tank has an air-injecting device to ensure intensive washing. The film dryer has a dust-filter. The dryer can be

fixed to wall, or to bench. Cost
restricts their use to a community
darkroom.

Thermometers

A spirit thermometer is not
simple to hold or read. It is easy
to break. Floating or dial types
may be less accurate, but are
tougher; the luminous head gives
a clearer reading. Electronic
models are precise, and give a
luminous, digital readout. You can
also buy an angled dish
thermometer. The dial is angled
for reading.

Print Processing

While it is acknowledged that
there are problems which relate to
print processing, such as using
tongs, there is no section on the
subject included in this book since
most print processing these days,
unless for high quality exhibition
work, is on resin coated paper
and this is easily dried by being
hung on a line.

CHAPTER FOURTEEN : PHOTOGRAPHY FOR BLIND AND VISUALLY DISABLED PEOPLE

The Royal Blind School, Edinburgh has recently introduced a course on the practice of photography. The course was seen as important in 'countering stereotyped ideas of what blind people can or cannot do.' For the students it was hoped that photographs would introduce a new dimension of visual stimulus. There were also plans to experiment with producing Minolta tactile copies of some of the photographs. The cameras used were of a 'rangefinder' fixed lens type, whilst a single lens reflex camera was used for studio work. In the darkroom measuring was aided by the use of a talking thermometer and jugs with raised level indicators. Contact sheets were examined with the aid of x8 magnifiers. When all the contact sheets were studied the students selected about forty images to enlarge over the final two weeks of the course. Some of these were photocopied and put through the stereocopying process to produce raised images. The photographs and raised images were combined in a montage, mounted on a card.

Problems with camera shake were not greater than they are for all beginners in photography.

Focusing the enlarger proved to be more difficult. Julie Rattray and Clare Pitkeathly write: 'Taking the pictures we found relatively easy but what was most interesting was the developing and enlarging of the prints. We found that to see our work filled us with a great sense of achievement.' [1]

The problem with focusing the enlarger could be solved by purchasing an automatic enlarger, which, although more expensive, is now freely available second hand.

Photography for blind and visually disabled people is orientated towards the darkroom and enhancement of visual awareness rather than adaptation of equipment. In the past, the tendency has been to treat people with low vision as though they cannot see, rather than to develop what they can see. In fact, most registered blind people do have some vision.

In the darkroom experimentation can take place and development of darkroom techniques produces modification and isolation of visual elements to facilitate seeing. [2] Photograms for example, provide a means whereby a physical object can be explored, not by touch alone, but by means of a bright same size reversed image, which precisely identifies the contours of that object.

Discoveries are often made during printing, such as the discovery of a friend standing in the background forming on the print who was previously unnoticed when the photograph was shot. In this way, configuration, confused through the viewfinder while shooting, can be examined and interpreted. This 'capturing' of visual information feeds visual curiosity, and frequent use of the darkroom develops 'latent vision'.

The blind American photographer George Covington took up photography because he wanted to see what his friends look like: 'Other people see to photograph; I photograph to see'.

Covington presents methods for using photography to see everything from works of art to architectural design and the faces of friends: 'In many cases photography can do more for a person with low vision than an operational or optical aid.' In his view, photography is such an effective tool for visually disabled people because a photograph is a 'high contrast abstraction of reality that reduces thousands of contours, shapes, hues and textures to a few shades between black and white wherein confusing shapes and distances become two dimensional objects'. [3]

In the words of another American photographer: 'The best part was my awareness of how much I could see of a friend's face, a beautiful fall day or a work of art through my observations of the many pictures taken.' [4]

High Contrast Abstraction
There are a number of darkroom techniques which are particularly useful in producing high contrast abstraction

Line Film

Normal photographic paper gives a continuous tone image; a range of greys between black and white. To produce a stark line image in black and white only, line film should be used.

Photograms

Photograms are made without using a camera. You place an object or objects on light sensitive paper and make an exposure. Opaque objects are seen as sharply defined shapes with hard line edges. Semi-transparent objects give a range of grey tone. A photogram gives negative tone values.

Tone-Line

Tone-line converts a continuous tone photograph into a white or black contour image, not unlike ink drawing.

Prints With Unusual Bases

These bases accentuate the contrast between background and foreground.

Luminous Photographs

Photographs can be made to glow in the dark. Coat a sheet of plain paper with luminous paint and expose negative under the enlarger. A glowing image will be visible in the dark.

Photographs on Silver

As the base will show a metallic surface instead of white, the image is enhanced in all its detail. Black images will show up in contrast to the silver.

Blocking Out

Sometimes you may wish to modify the background of the picture to make the main image stand out. The simplest method is to paint all secondary areas white . This is done by 'blocking out' the print with an opaque medium. The blocked-out area gives sharp definition to the image and a true line to follow. This would then be re-photographed.

Magnification

Close Up

The simplest way to take close-up photographs is to move as close as you can to the subject. The standard lens on a 35mm SLR camera will focus as close as 0.5m, which is close enough to record, say, a tree bud bursting into leaf.

Supplementary Lenses

The next simplest, is to add close-up supplementary lenses. There are no exposure adjustments necessary.

You can use a macro lens for really close-up work. It offers good quality, but is expensive. These lenses cannot be used by anyone who has difficulty in focusing.

Reversing Rings

For greater magnification you can put a standard lens into the camera the wrong way round. The lens is attached to the camera by a reversing ring which screws into the lens thread and the camera body. With the lens reversed manual control of the aperture is required.

Magnifiers

Magnifiers mounted on a headband leave hands free for other jobs in the darkroom. A large range of magnifiers is available, some with extra lenses, which swivel round to increase magnification.

Alternatively, there are stand magnifiers with a flexible arm or an ordinary magnifier can be held in a position with a double-ended clamp with a flexible arm. This equipment should be on sale at most opticians.

A photographer, in his seventies, continued his hobby, by using a similar magnifier, after losing his sight. His vision meant he could differentiate between light and dark. Unable to take in the complete picture, a watchmaker's glass allowed him to study the printed result of his work.

W.K.Corneck, writing to Oculus magazine, states: 'I carry a pocket 110 camera whenever I go "sightseeing" to take a snap, which, when printed in the now standard large print, I can study in detail with my magnifier at home, and thus enjoy the scene and detail of the place I have visited.' [5]

Focusing

The modern automatic SLR camera has solved most of the problems traditionally associated with focusing.

The standard manually operated 35mm SLR camera with adjustable controls presents problems where ability to focus is critical. Adjustable aperture controls affect amount of 'sharp zone', (i.e. depth of field), which is extent of ground from foreground to infinity in sharp focus. When settings have to be estimated, it is useful to change to a short focal length lens because of the extended depth of sharp focus. Use of a short focal length lens, (set at f8), with autoexposure, achieves a reasonable extent of 'sharp zone'.

rangefinder camera. You may be able to obtain a rangefinder camera, or the separate rangefinder, out of the equipment collected by the Disabled Photographers's Society, (address, p14); but only if you are a member.

Rangefinder
(Fig 59)

A rangefinder type camera is particularly helpful for people with low vision. The rangefinder makes the camera more easy to focus, than, say, split image. Two, separate, overlapping images can be seen when the subject is out of focus. Adjusting the focus ring brings the two images together. When they are in register, they are in focus. The built-in rangefinder camera, of course, presents a reduced image of the subject. (Fig. 59).

The rangefinder was originally a separate piece of equipment, with a dial on the back which would give the range. The two images seen through the viewfinder which have to overlap, are larger scale than in a

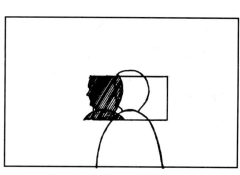

Out-of-focus image

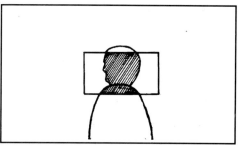

Focused image

DIRECT VISION RANGEFINDER CAMERA

Fig. 59

Sportsfinder
(Fig 60)
Most viewfinders reduce the size of the image you are looking at. A wire frame sportsfinder is designed to give the same view as would be seen if using the viewfinder itself, only full size. It does not, however, give you distance. The advantage is that, as the finder is not coupled to the lens; you look direct at the action. Different masks are fitted to the frame according to the focal length of the lens. (Fig.60).

Correction Lens
If you wear glasses, focusing may present problems, as they have a tendency to touch the back of the camera or mist up just at the wrong moment. There are

Fig. 60

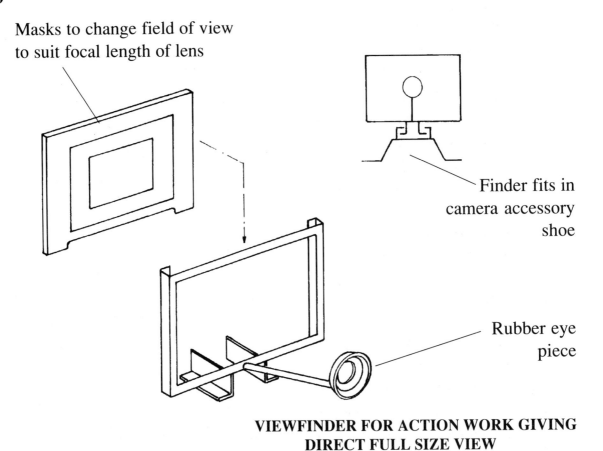

Masks to change field of view to suit focal length of lens

Finder fits in camera accessory shoe

Rubber eye piece

VIEWFINDER FOR ACTION WORK GIVING DIRECT FULL SIZE VIEW

special eye pieces available to counteract this. Alternatively, you can fit an eyesight correction lens to the viewfinder made up to an optician's prescription.
(See pp.40, 41, Fig.8).

Eyecups

It may be difficult to see the subject in very bright conditions. A rubber eyecup fitted to the viewfinder will keep out unwanted light.

Relief Guide

For many visually disabled people vision is not a matter of what they can see but of what picture they can build up in the mind's eye, of person, or of place. To look with information may be 'to see' whereas, to look without information may be not 'to see'.

The Minolta Stereo Copying Developing Unit (£2,500 approx.) makes raised tactile representations of visual images. It is important to use a suitable high contrast diagram or photograph. The image is photocopied and then fed into a preheated stereo copier. All black parts of the image, (depending on density reading), are raised to produce a contour effect. The Unit requires special paper called 'Micro Pearl'. These are sold at cost by Minolta; (200 sheets A4 £58). [6]

Personal Computers

Personal computers can be used to 'process' photographic images. The basic equipment consists of: a computer with a high resolution monitor, a scanner and an appropriate software package.

A photograph or transparency is scanned into the computer where it can be 'developed' in a variety of ways, by using:

(i)   a keyboard

(ii)   a 'mouse' (a small device which is operated by hand)

(iii)   voice commands; special software enables the user to programme the computer to respond to a set of verbal commands

(iv)   touch screens; specialised monitors which display information and transmit signals via a touch sensitive screen.

The 'developed' print can be printed out as a line, tone or half-tone photographic image.

The price of this equipment is outside the range of most people's pockets, (£2,000, upwards), but hopefully not of all community organisations. [7]

Tapes

At a photography exhibition, a taped commentary - available on a Walkman type cassette - is not only desirable, but necessary; not just from the visual perspective, but in order to reveal the motivation of the photographer, which though not a visual element of the photograph, is only inferrable from it visually. (A magnifying lens, by allowing you only a small area of the photograph at a time, denies you an overall 'view'. A taped commentary can supplement this.)

Contacts

RNIB,
224 Great Portland St
London W 1
N6AA.Tel:0713881266

Royal National College For The Blind,
College Rd,
Hereford. HR1 725
Tel: 0432 265 725

Partially Sighted Society,
Valley and Vale,
Leisure Centre,
Gibbonstown,
Barry,
South Glamorgan
Tel: 0446 742289

The Disabled Photographers' Society, (address, p 14).

You might also approach William Kirby, who is a specialist consultant on art and blind and visually disabled people.
11 Eastgate St,
Winchester SO23 8EB

CHAPTER 15 : PHOTOGRAPHY
AND DISABLED PEOPLE

Imagine a simple transaction: a disabled photographer contacts a local engineer with a view to adapting a camera to their use. They meet and discuss the problem and as a result of this through mutual consultation they modify a camera together. A relationship is established and gradually the photgrapher builds up a stock of equipment for their personal use in collaboration with the engineer. The photographer is keen to pass on to others the benefits gained both from the joint experience and from the stock of equipment.

This sort of information is the stuff of a manual on photography and disability. Yet no book on Photography and disability would be complete without introducing some of the debates which revolve around disabled people and the arts today and ending segregation. According to the Arts Council report, 'Photography and Disability in England', (1990), [1] these debates can be divided into two broad areas: arts and disabiltiy and disability arts.

In a keynote article on 'Disabled People and our Culture Development', based on a speech at the LDAF, (London Disability Arts Forum), Vic Finklestein explains the meaning of disability culture: 'the normal (able-bodied) world has lost sight of disabled people and our view of the world.' Real integration', he believes, 'can be achieved on the basis of a full recognition of our differences and this in turn will depend a great deal on us making a free choice to identify ourselves as a social group....there is already an identity developing amongst ourselves with our own cultural expression....It must develop spontaneously and creatively out of the collective experiences of disabled people....the willingness of disabled people to present a clear unashamed self identity and our ability to organise our own effective organisations for social change will greatly help the development of a disability culture.' [2]

The nature of disabilty arts has been described recently by Elspeth Morrison in a handbook: 'Policy into Practice: Disability'. [3] 'Disability arts is an expression of disability culture.' In the same way that other minority groups have their culture, so do disabled people. Disability arts is about: 'a range of art forms created *by* rather than *for* disabled people....Disability arts acknowledges that disabled people are disabled and work produced is *because of* not *in spite of* the disabilities'. [3]

As is pointed out in the Arts Council report: 'It is the common identity of living with disability-oppression that is the mainstay of this arts movement.'

Bob Findlay in an article entitled, 'In Defence of the Crippled Body', identifies this oppression: 'Disability is....about denying people their right to be regarded as equal and respected members of society. People who experience disability are sick and tired of able-bodied people speaking and acting....on our behalf.' [2]

Alan Sutherland remarks: 'We don't see our disabilities as obstacles that we have to overcome.' Again: ' And stories about how dreadful it is to be disabled value being able-bodied not disability.' [2]

An organiser at one conference, talking about art, observes: 'Artists with disabilities are not considered to be real artists....either the media are interested in how we do the work - with our toes, or with our tongues, and not the content, or it is considered therapy.' [4]

Disability arts may consist, the report states: 'at its extreme, of work that could not be physically produced by a non-disabled person (photography as seen by someone with a specific visual impairment for example, or using muscle spasm to create a particular photographic quality).'

The arts and disability approach is summed up in the report as contained in the attitude: 'We think of a person as an artist first, disabled second - its ability that counts....The focus here is on an individuals' impairements rather than viewing disability as an oppression'. Presumably, the object of the focus is to put a disabled person in the same position as they would have been had they not been disabled. It may be by use of a brush holder fitted to the lower teeth by a dentist or a mechanical adaption for a camera, etc.

This indicates how fuzzy the boundary can be between arts and disability and disability arts. An artist who uses a brush holder in order to paint, in the nature of the process, produces a work that a non-disabled person could not physically produce; unless as a conceit. In other words the adaption enables them to produce work that is inherently disability art. But a disabled photographer, using a mechanical adaption will be in a position to produce work that puts them in the same position as a non disabled photographer; in other words to produce work *in spite of* their disability.

The provision of adaptions by non-disabled people does not necessarily put that activity in the area of either arts and disability or disability arts. The test is how a disabled artist uses an adaption.

A feeling that disabled people are made not uncommonly to have is: 'being guilty for being here in the first place'. Both the following extracts are from letters from community projects in response to an enquiry about their resources for disabled people. Both by using isolating language and concentrating on ability indicate how this feeling can be implanted.

A project worker lamenting 'Just how little we do', writes: 'I would also like to point out that there are alternatives to conventional photographic work, I'm thinking of using "low-tech" resources such as "pin-hole cameras", old box cameras and working solely with light intensive materials, all of which are particularly appropriate to the disabled.' Who are 'the disabled'? Are they an alien species who land at night, come into our homes and steal our cameras?

A workshop manager writes: 'The darkroom is rather on the small and unmanoeuvrable side. To my knowledge we have never tried to accomodate a wheelchaired person in the darkroom, but I imagine that with a bit of thought it would be possible.'

It is not disabled people that are unmanouevrable but the unmanoeuvrability of non disabled people's attitudes. Does a

'wheelchaired person' have
wheels as part of their anatomy?
In such statements segregration
is implicit.

As Mandy Colleran states:
'The word segregation itself is a
verb, so its to "segregate". That
means that somebody is doing it
to you, you're not doing it
yourself. You have to be a
"segregate" or whatever, you
have to *be* segregated.' She
continues: 'The word that we
should maybe use now as
disabled people, is, "separatism",
that is, a choice to be separate,
one doesn't have a choice to be
segregated, but one can choose
to be separate.' [2]

How can we expect to hold a
dialogue when our own language
makes us strangers in a land with
such strange vegetation as kerbs,
steps, knobs, doors, escalators,
bus platforms, etc? The words
we use disassociate. The same
words express thoughts that put
us in the allotment.

And so it comes about that the
simple transaction described at
the beginning of this chapter is
interrelated to many other less
simple transactions.

ACKNOWLEDGEMENTS

This book by the time of going to publication will already in some details be out of date. It cannot be guaranteed that all membership fees, courses are correct, every organisation referred to in existence, their facilities at that time are unchanged, or any piece of equipment still on the market at that time.

Chapter 1:

[1] *Arts and Disabled People*. The Attenborough Report, 1985. Carnegie United Kingdom Trust. Bedford Sq. Press, p3.

[2] *A Survey of Initiatives in Great Britain concerning Arts and Disability*. Rod Fisher. The Rockefeller Foundation, May 1983.

Chapter 2:

[1] *REMAP* Yearbook, 1989.

[2] The map is taken from *REMAP* Yearbook, 1989.

[3] AIM is now Merseyside Disability Arts Forum

Chapter 3:

[1] We owe the information in these paragraphs to Mr P.Stroud of the Disabled Photographers' Society.

[2] Addresses of REMAP panels referred to in this and subsequent chapters may be obtained from the National or Regional Organiser REMAP. (See p.15).

[3] Where to Buy a Camera in London
The two main photographic equipment retailers in London are:
LEEDS CAMERAS: Brunswick Square, 071 833 1661
KEITH JOHNSON AND PELLING:
Drummond St NW1, 071 380 1144
KEITH JOHNSON AND PELLING:
Great Marlborough St W1, 071 439 8811

Both dealers will give advice on available equipment; both have extensive second hand departments; *KJP* has a service and repair departments.

*SECOND-HAND EQUIPMENT CAN ALSO BE BOUGHT
FROM: FOX TALBOT*: Tottenham Court Rd, 071 387 7001
FOX TALBOT: The Strand, 071 379 6522
MORGAN: Tottenham Court Rd, 071 636 1138
LEOPOLD: Tavistock Place (a small professional dealer with a small stock of cheaply-priced but well-used ex-professional equipment)
CAMPKINS: Frognal Parade, Finchley Road, 071 435 1227
JESSOPS: Finchley Road, 071 794 8786
CITY CAMERA EXCHANGE: High Holborn, 071 405 3364
CITY CAMERA EXCHANGE: Canon St. Station, 071 623 1381
LONDON CAMERA EXCHANGE:
Waterloo Station, 071 928 9795

Most of the above and many second-hand equipment dealers outside London advertise weekly in the back pages of the Amateur Photographer. The classified ads in this magazine are also worth looking at. We are grateful to Philip Wolmuth for supplying this list.

Chapter 5:
    [1]   The Brighton panel has no working drawings of this arrangement. The drawing is our reconstruction.
    [2]   Knut Aase can be contacted through The London Print Workshop. Patent of the design is pending.

Chapter 6:
    [1]   Nick Burton can be contacted through The London Print Workshop.
    [2]   Technical information sheet: Benbo Tripods.
    [3]   This design may be obtained from the Information Officer, Disabled Living Foundation. Camera Aid: List 8, 'Leisure', 80/13.
    [4]   Marketing Report: B.Ed (Hons) Urban Technology Project, 1987. Thames Polytechnic Incorporating Avery Hill College, Avery Hill Campus, Bexley Rd, S.E.9 2PQ, Tel 081 316 8000.

Acknowledgements

Chapter 8:
   [1]   Cartoon reproduced with the kind permission of *Punch*.

Chapter 10:
   [1]   Figs 46-48 are based on photographs of the former CLIC darkroom at Flower Lane.

Chapter 11:
   [1]   *Fujimoto (UK) Ltd,*
         Broad Hinton, Swindon,
         Wiltshire, SN4 9PA
         Tel: 0793 73 666/7

Chapter 12:
[1]   *Drager Ltd,*
         The Willows, Mark Rd,
         Hemel Hempstead.
         Hertfordshire. HP2 7BW.
         Tel: 0442 3542.

Chapter 13:
   [1]   Film drying idea: Phil Ridler.

Chapter 14:
   [1]   *Art To Share*, Photography Workshop: Rob Hoon & Margarette Burns Finlayson. *New Beacon* October, 1989.
   [2]   *'An Introduction to "Vision of the Inner Eye"'*, an exhibition at Oxford Polytechnic, 1987.
   [3]   G. Covington News Release, Smithsonian Institution, 1984.
   [4]   Marcus Weisen, RNIB, has provided useful material for this chapter.
   [5]   *Oculus* (March/April,1987)
   [6]   We are grateful to Margarette Burns Finlayson of the Royal Blind School, Edinburgh for the information on the Stereo Copying Developing Unit.
   [7]   J.Phillips.

[7]   J.Phillips.

Chapter 15:
[1]   *Photography and Disability in England* : Arts Council, 1990.
[2]   The quotes in this section numbered [2] are drawn from various
      issues of DAIL Magazine, (Disability Arts in London). The
      citation from Natalie Markham: DAIL 37. The article by
      Vic Finklestein:*'Disabled People and Our Culture Development'*:
      DAIL 8.
      Contact : *Elspeth Morrison, Disability Arts in London,
      c/o Artsline, 5 Crowndale Road, London. NW1 1TU
      Tel: 071 388 2227.*
[3]   *Policy into Practice: Disability.* Elspeth Morrison,
      Independent Theatre Council, 1990.
[4]   *A Survey of Initiatives in Great Britain concerning Arts and
      Disability.* Rod Fisher. The Rockefeller Foundation, May 1983.

NOTES

NOTES